ACTION FOR
CHANGE

COMMUNITY ACTION FOR CHANGE

Ray Lees and Marjorie Mayo

Routledge & Kegan Paul

London, Boston, Melbourne and Henley

First published in 1984
by Routledge & Kegan Paul plc

39 Store Street, London WC1E 7DD, England

9 Park Street, Boston, Mass. 02108, USA

464 St Kilda Road, Melbourne,
Victoria 3004, Australia and

Broadway House, Newtown Road,
Henley-on-Thames, Oxon RG9 1EN, England

Set in Sabon 10/12 pt
by Columns of Reading
and printed in Great Britain
by The Thetford Press Limited, Thetford, Norfolk

Library of Congress Cataloging in Publication Data

Lees, Ray.
Community action for change.
Bibliography: p.
Includes index.
1. Community development – Great Britain. 2. Public
welfare – Great Britain. 3. Social action – Great Britain.
4. Evaluation research (Social action programs) – Great
Britain. 5. Socialism – Great Britain. I. Mayo, Marjorie.
II. Title.
HN400.C6L43   1984   361.8   83-24478

ISBN 0-7100-9743-3

Contents

Acknowledgments

This book has emerged from discussions over the years with a great many people in the community work and community action field. Whilst these are too many to name personally, the work of the community resource centres used in the illustrative case studies must be acknowledged particularly. The case studies were first published as a report to the European Economic Community and our colleague Nick Bailey at the Polytechnic of Central London took a large part in the research and preparation of this volume. Of the present book, Marjorie Mayo has brought together the case studies in co-operation with community activists in the various areas. Ray Lees is responsible for the introduction and the discussion of community action and party politics, whilst the authors have worked together on the subsequent interpretation and central themes developed in argument. Part of the work was funded through the Gulbenkian Foundation and we would like to thank in particular our steering committee at that time which was chaired by David Jones. While we have received much help and support in the research programmes that have provided material for this book, it must be made clear that the interpretation, arguments and conclusions are the responsibility of the present authors alone. We must also thank Pyp Hall, who typed many drafts before the manuscript was finally completed.

Introduction
Socialism and community action

This book traces the development of community action in the past
two decades and discusses its significance for the Labour Movement,
with particular emphasis on recent case studies. A major goal
for a coalition of socialist interests in Britain must be to build a
public consensus in favour of socialist government that will
sustain radical policies in the direction of achieving a socialist
society. The growth in community action could be interpreted as
one important movement in this direction. A major obstacle to this
end, however, must be the political situation where something
between a quarter and a third of adult British workers consistently
vote Conservative rather than Labour. Despite the growth during
the 1970s of community groups that one might expect to be
sympathetic to socialist aspirations, the vote which swept Mrs
Thatcher and Sir Keith Joseph to power in 1979 recorded one of
the highest Conservative votes amongst industrial workers in
any post-war election, a victory which was not reversed in 1983,
even after the experiences of four years of Conservative cuts and
record levels of unemployment.

In fact, local Labour parties have not always sought to forge
links with community groups and some Labour councils have
been definitely hostile to radical community activities. In the post-
war era to some the Labour Party came to be associated more with
the growth of red-tape bureaucracy than the ideals of equality and
participatory democracy. That this lesson has begun to be learned
within the party can be seen in the changes being made in its
management and decision-making. The vicissitudes of everyday
politics will influence how the Labour Party changes and one must
certainly be cautious; even if it is the case that the Labour Party is
becoming more determined and realistic in its efforts to move
towards a socialist Britain, there remains the difficulty of gaining

the support of other constituencies. There is, therefore, a need for a broad everyday culture in favour of socialist policies.

People's ideas are not fixed and are particularly susceptible to the influence of everyday experience. One important way that this may happen is when people co-operate to work for change in a local situation. Such collective action will fail if motivated by utopian goals that do not take account of the wider structures in society, but practical programmes can bring gains. It is the grass-roots nature of such action that should make it attractive to socialist activists; it offers the opportunity to work towards building a socialist culture that will sustain the kind of change that cannot be achieved through parliamentary activity alone.

While the notion of 'loss of community' has a long and contentious history in the writing of social scientists and social philosophers, it reemerged in the 1960s as an important explanation for forms of social deprivation associated with run-down inner city and industrial areas. There followed in the United Kingdom an expansion of community projects and community work initiatives, such as the general community initiatives sponsored by the Urban Programme or the more experimental pilot projects such as the Community Development Projects Programme and the Comprehensive Community Programme. The present book combines research evaluating the most recent efforts in this field, community resource centres sponsored by the Gulbenkian Foundation, the Home Office and the EEC (completed in 1981) with an assessment of the various and sometimes divergent community initiatives that have occurred during the 1970s and into the 1980s.

Since the late 1960s political life in Britain has been increasingly influenced by movements for grassroots participation and an emphasis on community action. On both the left and right there have emerged criticisms of large scale local government bureaucracies and the hitherto prevailing consensus concerning the welfare state. But although they have common roots in calling for more community activity at local level, left wing emphasis on community action operates on different assumptions from the right wing demand for more self-help and voluntary effort. This book discusses how these changes have occurred and looks at their significance for the new political patterns that are emerging in the 1980s. As well as drawing on published sources to draw out theoretical and practical implications, our discussion will be illustrated from our own recent research evaluating government-sponsored community projects that formed part of an EEC anti-poverty programme.

As the British political scene moves increasingly into a state of flux, it is our purpose to illustrate not only what has been happening over a range of community activities but also to draw out lessons that can be learned at a time of apparently increasing uncertainty and lack of confidence in the stability of our social system.

Looking back from the economic and political situation of the early 1980s, the explicit aims and objectives and theoretical assumptions of officially sponsored community development and anti-poverty programmes of the early to mid seventies may seem, on first consideration, to be characteristic of a bygone era. The prevailing consensus of the notions of politicians from both the major parties in Britain, as well as from many of their academic and professional consultants outside government, focused upon the contribution which such programmes could make to improved and more cost effective social service delivery, coupled with the injection of a new lease of life into democratic mechanisms, particularly at the local level.

Community work was officially sponsored, it was suggested, for its capacity for:[1]

> affecting the course of social change through forming social relationships with different groups to bring about desirable change, . . . helping to relate the activities of service agencies more closely to the needs of the people they serve . . .
> and facilitating citizen participation to give 'life to social democracy'.

This was in fact the working definition of community work which was adopted for launching the community resource centres' programme which is the subject of this book.

In the present context, by comparison, the material problems of the deprived and the 3.3 million currently unemployed raise economic and political issues of an altogether different order. Even if production begins to recover in the early eighties, unemployment is expected to continue to remain high – as the employment secretary has commented: 'I think we in Britain are going to live with higher unemployment than we have experienced in the 50s or 60s' (Hansard, 24.4.81).

The welfare state itself has been undergoing no minor reorganisation but a restructuring process which in scope and ultimate implications could parallel the very process of industrial reorganisation. The political order has become more recognisably altered, too, with the end of the post-war 'Butskellite' cross-party support for Keynsian economic management strategies, combined with a mildly redistributive orientation for social welfare policies. So, both the major political parties have contained increasingly vocal protagonists of more extreme positions, whilst the 'middle-ground' in turn has been attempting to reformulate itself in response. Meanwhile, as part of the rationalisation of public spending, the balance between central and local government has been decisively altered too, through the effects of legislation, such as the Local Government and Planning Act, representing as it does a shift which has crucial implications for the potential success of any community action strategy aimed at the local, rather than the national political level.

In such an increasingly polarised political and economic scenario, what relevance could the milder, incremental community programmes of the previous decade continue to hold? If these programmes had indeed remained tied to the official pluralist definitions of the early seventies, they may indeed have been of historical interest only. But, in practice, the community pro-grammes of the past decade were typically more problematic, and as soon as the inherent, underlying conflicts of aims, objectives and theoretical assumptions of these community programmes are examined, their continued potential relevance can begin to become apparent, both in terms of their potential continued relevance for those on the right, and in terms of their relevance for those on the left of the social democratic middle-ground.

The first chapter looks at the relationship between community action and party politics over the past two decades and the different practices that were adopted in relation to the community field. Chapter 2 considers the nature of these debates in more detail, tracing different approaches to community development, for example, the focus upon community-based social control, and the attempts to effect a major shift from public to voluntary community care-based service provision, as contrasted with the focus upon challenging official approaches and definitions of poverty and deprivation and building organisations and organisational links between working people in their separate spheres of work and home, production and social reproduction.

These attempts to develop class- rather than simply community-based politics were part of a wider movement to alter the terms of the contemporary political status quo. Current debates about the possibility of democratising the Labour Party both at local and national levels can be traced, too, in some of these earlier concerns in the community development/community action debates about the goal of revitalising local democracy.

The threads of these debates which underlie the apparently more consensual definitions of community work in the early 1970s run throughout this book. And as these conflicts sharpened in the political and economic context of the latter part of the decade at national level, so the conflicts sharpened too, in terms of the alternative strategies to be pursued by community workers and community activists.

This particular study is concerned with a set of community resource centres which were only one aspect of community work intervention over this period, but they were a typical aspect all the same, at least in so far as they contained within their experience the substance of these wider debates and dilemmas. Chapter 3 locates the resource centres' programme within this context of community work in Britain, and anti-poverty programmes more generally.

The second section of this study is concerned with these debates as they emerged through the specific instances of the area resource centres example.

In the case studies dealing with the resource centres' work on providing information and advice, employment and housing, for example (Chapters 4, 5 and 6), the outlines of these contemporary community work and community action controversies can be traced, in more detail, in relation to the wider context.

In the concluding chapter, however, we return to some of the implications for the wider debates about the alternative prospects for community work and community action, and for their possible bases of support and funding in the 1980s.

Finally, as the discussion has already begun to touch upon the conclusions, the reader may be wondering about the omissions, the whereabouts of the sections of race and women. After all, it has become a commonplace that the 'community' is in some senses the specific sphere of women, the location of struggles around social reproduction which involve women in their domestic roles, both as the front-line consumers as well as the front-line field workers of the welfare state's services. As Elizabeth Wilson, for example, has argued, community work and the women's movement grew from the same upsurge of political consciousness and operated on the same terrain, attempting to grapple with the problems of urban industrial life – the politics of everyday life. Both share common theoretical concepts and perspectives and both have been crucially concerned with the role of the state and more specifically the welfare state, in terms of its concerns to facilitate the processes of social reproduction.

At one level, women do indeed emerge, chapter by chapter, throughout this study, at least as front-line consumers of the welfare state. For example, women are disproportionately at risk of dependence upon the social security system: some three-quarters of the adults dependent upon supplementary benefit are women (whether as pensioners, widows, or single parents). This ratio was mirrored, for instance, in the study of the Tribunal Access Unit in Chapter 4, where the majority of the claimants interviewed were, not surprisingly, women.

Women's responsibilities for and concern with health care has also been identified, whether as the elderly or, more typically, as childbearers and mothers of young children. And once again, those who attended the community health sessions (see Chapter 4) were virtually all women. The tenants' organisations which the resource centres in Manchester, South Wales and Tyne and Wear supported, for example, were similarly virtually exclusively composed of women; housing had indeed effectively been defined as the women's proper sphere of concern in these areas.

Women's involvement in housing issues, and the impact of their collective experiences, emerge more specifically in Chapter 6. Here, women activists in the South Wales Association of Tenants discuss the positive changes in their consciousness of themselves as women, and the consequent adjustments and eventual improvements in their personal relationships as a result of their involvement in community action. There women activists involved in the North East Tenants' Organisation were similarly aware of developments in their consciousness of themselves as women, as well as in their social and political consciousness more generally.

Chapter 5, on employment issues, also looks at women's

employment and at attempts to redress the balance in relation to initial community-based approaches to the jobs question. Until the emergence of feminist projects and women's employment it has, in fact, been argued[2] that the increasingly critical focus upon employment work has actually reinforced this neglect of women's issues (the job issue being defined typically as men's work, the productive sphere, despite the fact that nearly half the labour force is female).

But overall women's issues were not raised systematically enough from a feminist perspective in the projects in the case studies, even within women's so-called 'special sphere of the community', simply because of the relevance of the issues or their common theoretical bases. On the contrary, in general there have been powerful pressures in the opposite direction – pressures which have been challenged only as the result of quite specific and conscious struggles by feminists. These factors, then, are part of the explanation, although certainly not the justification for the relative invisibility of women, until the final case study.

The other aspect of these omissions, race, is even more seriously absent, and this is particularly so in the case studies. This is all the more surprising at one level, in view of the early emphasis on race in community programmes and particularly upon racial tensions and the need to contain these through government-sponsored programmes for the inner city. Chapter 2, for example, touches upon these issues, together with some consideration of alternative approaches to black liberation[3] based upon an analysis of the roots of black oppression in the colonial past and in present contemporary metropolitan socio-economic structures.

While certain of the resource centres did specifically provide resources to ethnic minority groups, overall, the location and staffing of these centres meant that they did not make very particular contributions to black and Asian community groups. Once again, then, whatever their original frames of reference community programmes were failing to address this most central contemporary issue in practice. This can be expected to remain the key question for community work and community action programmes in the eighties.

We discuss these and related topics in our conclusions when we attempt to place action at community level in its contemporary context. The concept of community, perhaps because of rather than despite its ambiguities, remains a potent force in British political and social life. Our final task will be, therefore, to draw from our previous discussion what appear to be the advantages, limitations and pitfalls of this approach.

Part one
The relevance of community action

1 | The community action movement and party politics

Since the mid 1960s there has been a growth in community action of various forms. This has included the welfare rights movement, resistance against planning and redevelopment, the squatting movement, strategies to form alliances with trade unions, the local organisation of ethnic minorities, the development of feminist groups and demands for the devolution of decision-making in industry, politics and government. The guiding spirit of much of these developments has been the view that people should make decisions for themselves and have more control over their everyday environment. While people may have disagreed in detail about what needed to be done, there was agreement that existing arrangements were not satisfactory. In particular it was argued that the distribution of power and resources was both unjust and exploitative of many groups in society. There was also a distrust of large-scale bureaucracy and elitist political leadership. Though disparate and sometimes sectarian in their activities, their common emphasis on participatory involvement, changing consciousness and community action form part of what can be identified as an important social movement.

For our purposes we define a social movement, in broad terms, as a collective endeavour to promote change in the society of which it forms a part in a particular direction, but expressed in a general way without a detailed programme. A social movement is less organised than a political party and may have no regular and easily identifiable membership. As Bottomore pointed out:[1]

> Belonging to a movement is more a matter of sympathising with a particular social outlook or doctrine, expressing it in everyday political debate and being ready to participate in occasional activities such as demonstrations or 'riotous assemblies'.

Whereas organised political formations, such as parties, are directly engaged in the struggle for power, in the sense of seeking to return or capture the government of some political unit, social movements act in a more diffuse way and, if they are successful, establish preconditions for changes of policy or regime by bringing into question the legitimacy of the existing political system (in part or in whole), creating a different climate of opinion, and proposing alternatives.

Alongside the growth in community action that occurred in the mid 1970s there was also an increasing general estrangement and lack of confidence in conventional party politics. For example, Butler and Kavanagh in their study of the general election of 1974 claimed that 'there is much greater cynicism about the democratic process in 1974 than there was in 1945 when the first Nuffield election study was written.' The authors saw this growth in feelings of disillusionment as being largely due to the failure of governments[2]

> to satisfy the increasing expectations of the public. They are unable to solve the equation that confronts them, how to produce simultaneously full employment, stable prices, high rates of growth, increased social benefits and lower taxes. . . . The British government's supremacy, based on its power to pass laws through parliament, is seen by voters to be rather hollow when trade unions, or mass non co-operation, or events overseas can so obviously undermine and nullify its policies.

Certainly, to many people in 1974, the experience of two general elections in one year, failures in industrial relations, the presence of inflation, the problems of inner city areas, the prevalence of poverty, acts of political terrorism and perhaps a growing alienation to authority in society were indicative of a profound social malaise. For example, in the second election campaign of that year, politicians and commentators placed a great deal of emphasis upon the gravity of the situation. According to the Conservative Manifesto, the dangers facing Britain, both economic and political were 'greater than any since the last war',[3] the Labour Party acknowledged the 'most dangerous crisis since the war',[4] the Liberals pointed to 'a distinct lack of faith in government at the very time that it is most needed',[5] and *The Times* epitomised the general uncertainty in an editorial that asked, 'Can social democracy survive?'[6]

Writing in the early 1980s, social democracy is still surviving – but that is about all. With something like 3 to 4 million unemployed (more or less according to how you calculate the figures) combined with high rates of inflation, arresting and reversing Britain's economic decline has clearly become a gargantuan task. Conditions in inner cities have been another touchstone of crisis, grim enough to spark off riots in the summer of 1981 that produced images of fire, violence and looting on Britain's television screens, but riots that were rooted in an awareness of a lack of social justice. As politicians continue efforts at adapting to these ongoing problems, it can be shown that community politics, community action and populist appeals have been of considerable influence.

Not surprisingly there has been a reaction against the methods adopted by successive governments, which did not differ greatly until Mrs Thatcher came to power in 1979. The travails of both the Conservative and the Labour Parties, and the emergence of the Social Democrats in 1981, can be attributed either directly or indirectly to the belief that it was necessary to strike out in fresh directions. The direct influence of the community action movement can be illustrated most readily by the recent changes in the Labour Party, particularly in the constitutional changes that have occurred or for which demands are being strongly articulated. For many of the young people whose political passions and beliefs led them into community activism in the late 1960s and early 1970s have latterly joined in the struggle to transform the Labour Party into forms that are more directly democratic.

This development has been called by Webster a movement towards 'ultra-democracy'[7] in order to indicate that what is being demanded is the furthest possible downward extension of decision-making and the direct accountability of representatives to the grassroots of the party. Tony Benn has been the national Labour politician who most clearly articulated this demand for more popular participation in decision-making within the party. For example, while standing as a candidate for the deputy leadership of the Labour Party in 1981, Benn argued that:[8]

It is astonishing that members of the Labour Party and our

affiliated trade union members should have ever accepted a party constitution which excluded them from exercising any real responsibilty for electing the leadership in parliament, for re-selecting their own sitting MP or having an effective say in the policy put before the country in a general election. I also favour the extension of these principles to local government and the election of future Labour cabinets by Labour MPs.

Such changes modest as they are, will make the Labour Party leadership far more accountable to the membership. They will also strengthen parliamentary democracy and, I am sure, will be administered with our traditional tolerance and goodwill. They will also improve our credibility, because the voters will have reason to believe that what we say in opposition we will do in government.

There has always been the possibility and indeed typically the presence of tension between the parliamentary Labour Party and its constituency organisations as is evidenced in the traditional debate about the extent to which conference decisions should mandate Labour administrations. Hitherto, it has been argued that because of the way that prime ministerial government works with leadership coming from the cabinet, such conflict would almost inevitably end in victory for the parliamentary party.[9] Such victories have tended to ensure the pursuance of 'middle of the road' rather than more left-wing policies. Most recently the 1974-9 Labour government has been criticised in this way for not implementing the economic strategies that had been worked out in the early 1970s with an increased emphasis on state ownership and intervention, as well as for not pursuing other measures, such as the widespread introduction of industrial co-operatives and industrial democracy, the introduction of a Freedom of Information Act and the abolition of the House of Lords. The programme of constitutional changes (automatic reselection of MPs, widening the franchise for the election of the party leader, and the writing of the election manifesto by the national executive of the party) is intended, therefore, to make the parliamentary party much more responsive to party programmes that may originate and be supported outside of the parliamentary leadership. Labour leaders, it is argued, have in the past given too much compliance to the views of top businessmen, financiers, civil servants and Conservative politicians. Benn has succinctly stated, 'the discipline of the market place and the discipline imposed by the top people are both equally unattractive. We believe that the self-discipline of full democratic control offers our best hope for the future.'[10]

This vision of the future both complies with and emerges from the work of many community activists. During the 1960s and early 1970s many such people regarded the Labour Party as irrelevant and placed more emphasis on local groups than on banding together to advance their causes by joint political action, but in recent years community activists have started to see the party as a possible vehicle for advancing their causes in a common movement. The pressure for changes in the party's constitution has come, then, partly from activists such as council tenants, shop stewards, workers in the public sector and increasingly women and ethnic minorities – it is partly the product of what we have called the community action movement.

Of course, there has been and is resistance to these kind of changes within the Labour Party. For example, Denis Healey, the successful candidate for the deputy leadership in 1981, stated during his campaign:[11]

> The essence of democracy is the secret ballot and one man, one vote. . . . Too often, those who demand more democracy in the Labour Party want exactly the opposite – a system in which a small minority of self-appointed activists deny the vote to the average party member on the grounds that he is too idle or too susceptible to manipulation by the capitalist press to deserve it, and then deny their representatives the secrecy of the ballot so that they can terrorise anyone they disagree with. . . . In the Labour Party at present, this type of active elitism has succeeded in capturing some trade union branches, and has consolidated its gains by driving out the average party member by preaching sectarian hatred and by humourless beating of the ideological tomtom. But it is a hollow victory, since the Labour voter cannot be captured in this way.

Much of this kind of criticism against 'active elitism' has been directed against one faction of Trotskyists who decided upon 'entryism' into the Labour Party during the 1970s, organising themselves around a newspaper called the *Militant*. However, whatever view one takes of this organisation, and it can certainly be argued that some activists try to dominate rather than to facilitate participatory democracy, it is clear that the movement for constitutional change within the party has come from a broad front of activists and is not the product of any one sectarian group. As David and Maurice Kogan concluded in their detailed study of the non-Trotskyist Campaign for Labour Party Democracy, 'it would not have been possible for small groups of manipulators to have accomplished these changes without the support of many Labour Party members who perceived the leadership as oligarchic and distant'.[12] In the same way, the demand for more directly socialist measures has strong support within the party. Both demands reflect the experience of many people involved in the community action movement during preceding years.

Healey's second criticism relates to the attractiveness of the Labour Party to the wider electorate. Can a more directly democratic Labour Party with socialist policies win power at a general election? Faced with a Conservative government that has followed monetarist policies that have increased unemployment at a time of economic recession, one would expect an opposition party to be well placed to win power when the electoral opportunities arise. However, the defeat of the Labour Party in the 1983 election shows that this is far from being the case. Furthermore some sympathetic commentators believe that the possibility of further national electoral victory is becoming increasingly difficult. For example, Professor Hobsbawm, in a lecture given in 1978, put forward a substantiated argument for believing that the British Labour movement was now in crisis. Identifying a trend towards a shrinking Labour vote Hobsbawm pointed to underlying factors such as the changing occupational and class structure and the decline of the manual working class within it, to the growth of a large female workforce, to the growth of anti-immigrant feeling within the working class, and to a growing sectionalism in the trade union movement which 'at times actually set workers against each other rather than establish wider patterns of solidartiy'.[13]

Instead of working-class consciousness solidifying, it seems as fragmented as ever. There have always been 'differential workers' who have been Conservative supporters and Goldthorpe and

Lockwood have further identified 'privatised workers' as adopting an 'instrumental' attitude to work, society, the unions and Labour Party in their pursuit of affluence.[14] Certainly Mrs Thatcher's leadership of the Conservative Party in the 1979 election contained elements of a populist style that was anti-bureaucratic, favouring less taxation and bigger cuts in public spending. This electoral strategy was linked to demands for curbs on trade union power and greater concern with law and order when Mrs Thatcher observed that:[15]

> A trade union leader had advised his members to carry on picketing because they would act in such numbers that the authorities would need to use football stadiums as detention centres. This is the rule of the mob and not of the law, and ought to be condemned by every institution and minister in the land. The demand in the country will be for two things: less tax and more law and order.

The extent to which right-wing governments can appeal to working-class sentiment was further emphasised during the early stages of the Falklands crisis when the Conservative Party was consistently shown as gaining popularity in opinion polls, a development that was further reflected in the local government elections that took place at this time. This experience has shown that some of the dominant values of the nineteenth century, such as the desirability of a free-market economy, law and order and patriotic chauvinism, remain a potent political mixture in the 1980s, at least in the short term. Certainly policies based on these principles are leading to cuts in social services and accelerating economic decline. There seems no way in which the damage being done to the economy can be quickly or fully undone. On the basis of the effect of its policies, therefore, one would not have expected the Conservative Party to be in winning form for the 1983 election.

However, the formation of the Social Democratic Party and its electoral alliance with the Liberal Party meant that the electorate did not automatically turn to the Labour Party. The anti-Tory vote was in the 'majority', but it was split. It is clear that a great many people who had previously voted Labour chose not to do so in 1983. However, the success of the Alliance was more a measure of the low appeal of its rivals than of any evidence it has given of having any clear idea of how to cope with the nation's problems. Indeed the Social Democratic stance may be to avoid detailed programmes. As one of its leading figures, Professor Marquand, has written:[16]

> For, whatever may have been true in the 50's and 60's, 'moderation' is manifestly no longer enough. Britain's deepening economic and social crises cannot be overcome by the antiquated and backward-looking dogmas of the Bennite Left or the Thatcherite Right. Nor however can they be overcome by a soggy and apologetic centrism. Radical changes are needed in government, in industry, in the social services and in foreign policy. . . . Social Democracy offers no total conclusions, no magic formulas, no easy escapes from the perils and complexities of the late 20th century. It is a creed of provisional judgements, approximate truths, tentative conclusions.

It has been argued in this chapter that one of the connecting themes of various forms of community action is a belief in a high degree of participatory democracy and a distrust of large-scale bureaucracies. Some of this climate of opinion has had influence on all the parties though it has taken different forms of rhetoric: 'self-help', emphasis on small business and attacks on local government bureaucracies by the Conservatives; the 'community politics' that has been advocated by Liberals; the claim to be more democratic than traditional parties by the Social Democrats together with efforts to mobilise the middle classes and win the 'middle-ground'; and the efforts to make the Labour Party more directly democratic and to effect socialist policies that will produce structural change towards a more egalitarian society.

A broadly socialist programme will remain attractive to many community activists, but optimism as to whether the Labour Party can easily achieve this goal would be misplaced. The Labour Party's optimism in its early years rested on the assumption that in the end virtually all working people – in other words, the large majority of the population – would vote for the party. But, by 1979, only 28 per cent of those entitled to vote cast their votes for Labour. Underlying the loss of votes has been a decline in committed support for Labour politics and policies and a withering of Labour's roots in working-class communities. In 1983 fewer trade unionists, fewer women and fewer first-time voters supported Labour than at any post-war election. On the face of it, there is less public support for more public spending on welfare services, for extending nationalisation and a greater antipathy towards trade unions. But as the authors of *Manifesto: A Radical Strategy for Britain's Future* have pointed out:[17]

> The Social Democrats and their academic allies used such public opinion poll findings to argue that the party's Left wing was moving away from the party's supporters. Looked at more closely, the poll data suggests an alternative picture: support for more nationalization among Labour sympathizers did fall between 1964 and 1970, and from 1974-79, but it picked up noticeably up to 1974 after Labour's leadership swing behind the party's aggressive industrial policy with its emphasis on public ownership. Perhaps the unsurprising lesson really is that Labour supporters respond to what the party is telling them. Experience of Labour's leadership in government has continued, on the other hand, to erode traditional support.

But even in 1974 only half of the trade union voters who voted gave their votes to Labour. There is a problem, therefore, even given a parliamentary leadership more accountable and more dedicated to radical socialist policies, in obtaining and maintaining popular support for such measures. There is a need for grassroots activities to generate a broad alliance in local communities – groups such as ethnic minorities, tenants' associations, women, students, trade unionists and so on – in order to make parliamentary action possible and effective. From this point of view, community action and strategies should be linked to the Labour movement in a more critical way. To be effective, radical parliamentary policies need extra parliamentary support. The need to build a broad base of community support for socialist policies has been recognised by socialist writers and theoreticians. Much of this impetus has come from Marxist thinking influenced by Antonio Gramsci. When Gramsci was developing his own ideas he was particularly concerned about the success of the Fascist Party in gaining support from the working class in Italy during the 1930s. He argued that this was partly because of the failure of socialist ideals to become deeply rooted in the culture of working-class life and in the various institutions that have hegemony in the formation of ideas.[18] This same lesson must not be lost on the Labour movement in this country at the present time. In order to effectively tackle this problem a much stronger and dynamic community-based movement is essential.

It is in local politics that the community movement can make its first impact. It can be significant not only in propagating the theory of socialism, but also in demonstrating the possibility of practice; indeed it is the potential for combining theory and practice that is of greatest importance in developing a community action strategy – by people joining together to co-operate in groups, the processes of participatory democracy become a lived experience. But such activities must have goals which are also meaningful. Small-scale activities will not, in themselves, change the structure of society, but they can, nevertheless, improve the quality of everyday life as well as engender an awareness of the need for structural change.

The link between local democracy and the goals of socialism already has a tradition within the Labour movement. For example, Sidney and Beatrice Webb argued that local government could be seen as one of the agencies for the socialisation of the economy. The early history of the co-operative movement is a further example of a democratic joining together of consumers and producers. National policy at the moment is dominated by reliance on market forces with an extremely limited role for public intervention. There is a need to demonstrate that alternatives can be made to work and local democratic institutions form one basis for putting this into action.

One example where efforts have been made in this direction has been in the more innovative Labour-controlled local authorities. For example, in Sheffield, the city council is initiating plans for the economic reconstruction of the city in conjunction with local trade unions and local community groups. Similarly in London, the Greater London Labour Party is engaged in implementing a policy of joint consultation and local intervention. The initiators of such policies do not claim that capitalism will be transformed by such a series of local initiatives nor do they necessarily adopt what Michael Ward has called 'an a-theoretical romantic, "small is beautiful" approach'. Ward, himself a Greater

London councillor, has put the argument in the following way:[19]

> the lesson of the period since 1964 in particular must be that
> that national programme cannot simply be handed down from
> above: it must proceed on a basis of active campaigning
> support. In turn, this means that the elements of the
> programme need to be developed from below: industrial
> planning needs to come from the Labour movement and
> community organisations. That is the importance of the
> demand for accountability: accountability entails using the
> position of elected representatives to carry out the priorities
> determined by these organisations.

Of course, it is not simply in problems of production and
consumption that community initiatives can play a role in
developing a socialist perspective. Work with residents' associations, advice centres, pre-school playgroups, adventure play-
grounds, holiday play schemes, organisations representing ethnic
minorities, groups of single parents, women's groups, alternative
community experiments – all of these can include an important
socialist perspective for helping to build a grassroots socialist
culture. It is for this reason that the experience of community
work and community action during the 1970s is so important to
revitalising the Labour movement. It is to the experience of such
community initiatives that we will now turn.

There have been many instances of community action in the
history of working-class struggle, but it is to the late sixties and
early seventies that one turns in looking at the birth of the
contemporary community movement. Its roots are partly found in
the efforts made by radical students during that time to gain more
control over the way education was being conducted in univers-
ities. This began in the United States, partly as a reaction to the
Vietnam war, but also found expression in Europe reaching its
most dramatic success in France in 1968. Alongside this radical
demand for greater participation, control and accountability in
government, there developed an official response that also
emphasised a need for community involvement. This can be seen
in the American 'War on Poverty' initiated by Kennedy and later
developed by Johnson, a programme that emphasised the need for
'maximum participation' by the poor. In this country, a similar

response occurred with various reports emphasising the need for greater involvement in issues such as social work, education and planning, and was to find one of its main expressions in the setting up of government-sponsored community development programmes in the early seventies and the sponsorship of community initiatives through the Urban Programme. In both the American and the British cases it could be argued that these responses were a reaction to an increase in urban disorder and riots. Nevertheless, certainly in the British case, the community movement was to gain ground quickly.

By the early seventies three different strategies could be discerned that were significant in the community movement. One was concerned with gaining rights for underprivileged people. The welfare rights movement required community activists to be essentially representatives on behalf of and with the poor, arguing their case, obtaining their rights against unsympathetic bureaucrats, taking the lead in what Bull in 1970 called 'entitlement claims'.[20] What was required in addition to personal skills was legal knowledge and an awareness of entitlement in matters like supplementary and social security benefits, rent rebates, school meals, school uniforms, educational maintenance allowances and so on. The second strategy, commonly called community action, involved not only obtaining present rights but taking direct collective action to obtain an improved situation. Thus in King Hill in 1965, the residents and their husbands took over the running of a hostel for homeless families and forced reform on the authorities. The strategy there was to take action on a matter of common concern and then to challenge the authorities to resolve the conflict. The final variant, sometimes called community development, stresses participation as the means of achieving change without the polarisation of conflict inherent in community action. Such a view was implicit in the government-sponsored Community Development Project (CDP) Programme, where social workers and other officials were expected to activate a community so as to channel its ideas into constructive proposals – proposals that would be broadly acceptable to the authorities, although as we shall see CDP did not develop in the way that was thus anticipated.

Developments such as these differed not only in terms of overall strategies, but also in their aims. Problems manifest themselves differently to different groups in society and the solutions proposed also vary. To some militants participatory politics may be more important as a means of increasing political awareness than in achieving any particular piecemeal reform because their real goal is radical social change. In contrast the official sponsorship for community development rested on the assumption that in expressing and discussing problems, that is in articulating community need, it would become possible to resolve difficulties without open conflict. This was also the belief at least of some exponents of welfare rights; for example, Lynes (1969) described this movement as 'the new Fabianism', claiming that it seemed to offer a means of achieving 'gradual progress without changing the basic assumptions of our society'.[21] To put it another way, the revolutionary could be concerned with the politics of conflict for its own potential, while the reformer who may or may not make use of conflict strategies is essentially still looking for the politics of consensus through a new level of social awareness.

The original conception of CDP was one of carefully controlled experiment aimed at tackling conditions of social deprivation by improving service delivery, encouraging self-help and participation, experimenting with new ways of providing social welfare and combining the skills in research with action in order to monitor and evaluate this new departure in meeting needs. Such aims reflected certain concerns in social policy current at the time, such as positive discrimination through educational priority areas and the Urban Programme, greater co-ordination of welfare services through the post-Seebohm developments and more local participation in planning procedures following the Skeffington Report. Notions of self-help based on the idea of pathology existing in families with multiple problems were, however, quickly challenged from within CDP, culminating in the Interproject Report which stated that 'problems of multi-deprivation have to be redefined and re-interpreted in terms of *structural* constraints rather than psychological motivations, external rather than internal factors. The symptoms of disadvantage cannot be explained adequately by any abnormal predominance of individuals or families whose behaviour could be defined as pathological.'[22]

A further strategy developed out of the work of the CDP,

where some advocated the explicit forging of links between the workplace and the community, so that issues could be confronted on a broad base. North Tyneside CDP advocated a political organisation which would integrate people's experience and needs both at home and at work, while a later Interproject Report suggested that, with the increasing privatisation of society, brought about by a high level of permanent unemployment, it was imperative for the work of the Labour movement to focus on the community. This issue has subsequently been taken up by Coventry Workshop, which to some extent developed out of the work of Coventry CDP. The group has argued that:[23]

> The problems people face in their home environment have, at root, the same political and economic causes as the problems they face at the workplace. Effective action to win improvements in either situation requires a better understanding of the nature of the relationship between industry, the community, the economy and the state. . . . If people are to gain more control over the forces which affect their lives at work and at home, bridges will have to be built between trade unions and the community based organisations . . . (who) can use their power to exercise this kind of leadership on behalf of the whole community, but to be effective they will need new kinds of information and expertise.

The need to make connections between problems in the workplace and in the home has also been a central theme in the development of the women's movement. The development of the division of labour to the extent that production and reproduction appear increasingly as unconnected is a major obstacle to achieving equality between the sexes and, to be understood, certainly requires a community perspective.

It can be seen, therefore, that the concerns of socialist politics and the community movement have started to come together in a much more explicit form. On the one hand, there is the need for the Labour movement to engender a new enlivened constituency for its programmes. On the other hand, there is a need for these programmes to be much more concerned with community affairs. Of course, not all people involved in the community and voluntary organisations would wish to see this happen. Indeed, the community resource centre programme, on which we shall draw, itself derives mainly from a different tradition.

The proposal for both a national and an area resource centre came from a committee under the chairmanship of the late Lord Boyle, known as the Community Work Group (CWG), which, in 1979, published its report entitled *Current Issues in Community Work*.[24] The Boyle Committee started from a previous Gulbenkian Foundation report's definition of community work as consisting typically of 'work with groups of local people who have come into existence because they want to change something, or do something that concerns them. Community work also enhances attempts to relate the activities of social agencies more closely to the needs of the people they serve.' This process is essentially concerned with affecting the course of social change through the two processes of analysing social situations and forming relationships with different groups to bring about some desirable goal. Community work was also defined as facilitating and making more effective 'citizen participation'. In short, Boyle claimed 'community work is a means of giving life to local democracy.'

After a review of the way community work and action had grown in recent years, the concluding chapter of the Boyle Report identified areas of need in the community work field and proposals for meeting them. In the view of the Community Work Group the overriding focus of need lay in providing support for and fostering the development of emerging community groups, though this would include support for community work practitioners and teachers. It was also proposed that a national community development fund should be set up. From this perspective, the proposal for a national centre and for local resource centres was set out by Boyle in the following way:

Area centres should be set up within existing organisations, not necessarily within the same kind of organisation in each area. They should be in regular contact not only with local groups but also with the national centre. . . . The functions of these area centres would vary according to local needs and the services already available. Functions might include:

  (i) *Information*: to obtain and disseminate information of practical value to local workers and members of groups.
  (ii) *Supporting Services*: to provide professional and technical

  expertise whether as staff or consultants and training,
  especially in community work skills where necessary.
  (iii) *Equipment*: to provide a pool of resources for use by
  groups.
  (iv) *Opportunities for Discussion*: to provide facilities for
  meetings between members of different community groups
  in order to encourage discussions and the exchange of
  information and news.

With regard to funding, the report concluded:

  Funding should normally be a matter for the local authorities
  and voluntary organisations in the area (some are already
  beginning to provide such funds). But in order to establish the
  practical value of these centres, it might well be necessary to
  obtain from central government and trusts sufficient funds to
  promote experimental centres, preferably in, say, two very
  different areas, and to publish reports of their work.

It is important to make clear here that resource centres as
proposed by the Boyle Committee were never conceived as an
answer to, or as a direct attack on, material poverty or as a
poverty programme. They were never envisaged as a small area
approach to the resolution of poverty, but grew out of the wish to
stimulate community action by deprived populations and groups.
Nevertheless, the resource centre programme became funded by
and part of a larger European Economic Community 'anti-
poverty' initiative. It became, therefore, the product of government activity and subject to political judgment on its success or
failure, continuance or closure.

2 Community action and political theory

During the 1970s, as it has been suggested in the preceeding chapter, a series of debates took place both within the Marxist framework and outside it. Marxist critiques, in summary, provided a challenge to those within the laissez-faire and pluralist perspectives, as well as to those who were broadly in agreement over some, at least, of the starting assumptions of dialectical materialism.

The ensuing process of realignment and redefinition, especially in the latter half of the decade, would seem to contain at least two, apparently contradictory, elements. On the one hand, a process of polarisation has been traced, and an expansion of the boundaries of legitimate debate – the end of the Butskellite consensus, in theoretical terms, just as within the terms of the debate in the formal political arena.[1] So, by the 1980s, both Marxist and 'monetarist' approaches to the welfare state, for example, have become as legitimate as objects of study as the previously more prevalent forms of debate within the different sections of the pluralist perspective.

The deepening economic recession and the ensuing public expenditure cuts and attempts at public sector rationalisation by both Labour and Conservative governments in the second half of the seventies provided the background for these more theoretical attempts to develop 'radical' critiques, whether from the perspective of the radical right or from the left, or from progressive social movements such as the Women's Liberation movement.

However, it is also possible to trace a certain interest in re-establishing the 'consensus', albeit a reformulated consensus, shifted further along the pluralist continuum, by the pull of the 'radical right'. As it will be suggested subsequently in this chapter, there have been recent attempts to redefine the legitimate sphere of

27

community work which are consistent with precisely such a characterisation. It may be relevant to question, too, how far such attempts can be related to the growth of a political party based upon comparable goals (i.e., re-establishing some form of 'consensus politics' at the rightist end of the pluralist spectrum).

More generally, then, how far can such a framework for locating recent debates about socio-economic and political change be applied to debates about the purposes and the practice of community work? In this chapter, it will be suggested that the consideration of community work, by the very nature of its terrain, cannot be divorced from the discussion of precisely these wider issues, and that certain of the major themes within these wider debates have, indeed, been the key themes of debates within community work itself. This is, in no sense, to argue that community work possesses some unique centrality within the political process; on the contrary, in fact, while certain critics have persisted in emphasising the necessity for greater political modesty this criticism has continued long after it has, in practice, lost its validity. Community workers no longer claim to have any special pretensions in relation to political centrality, whether of a radical or indeed a repressive character.[2]

Community workers are, on the whole, only too conscious of the modesty of their potential professional contribution to the process of social change.[3] Without implying, then, that community work is, itself, the key, we shall suggest that elements within it are essentially linked to the political process and to the dynamics of political change, whether, for example, as an essential ingredient of pluralist democracy,[4] or as a necessary concomitant of the growth of corporatism in Western capitalist societies,[5] a rational feedback mechanism in the restructuring of the welfare state, or even as the precursor to alternative, socialist forms of welfare.[6]

To argue that community work is essentially political is in no sense to suggest that the politics of community work are fixed or unproblematic. On the contrary, community work has been sponsored and undertaken in relation to a range of different theoretical perspectives, mirroring the wider theoretical debates and political controversies of each period. And some of the most significant community work interventions have themselves contained mutually contradictory assumptions and policy goals. The

Home Office's national Community Development Project (discussed in Chapter 1) is perhaps the most obvious but by no means unique example of such inbuilt ambiguity.[7] Another example is the EEC's own involvement in community action via the anti-poverty programme, the sponsoring programme for the varying range of case studies discussed in Chapters 4, 5 and 6. There are, in fact, certain threads and themes within the community work debates which have been particularly susceptible to differential interpretations and emphasis, threads and themes which provide meeting points, or at least potential obfuscation points for the exponents of varying and/or conflicting theoretical perspectives.

Problematic concepts

The concept of participation has emerged, for example, from the previous chapter in this context. Already in the late sixties and early seventies the problematic nature of the concept was being discussed, both theoretically, in terms of alternative models of democracy[8] and in terms of alternative goals and outcomes. Has the concept of participation, then, been the property of pluralists, concerned to optimise the efficiency of feedback systems in the decision-making process, while at the same time gaining legitimacy for the ensuing policy decisions by incorporating the protests of the powerless? Or has 'participation' been defined as part of an alternative theoretical framework, in terms of the development of the collective organisation of the powerless and ultimately of their increasing collective strength to challenge the interests of the status quo, or even in terms of prefigurative forms of alternative models of participative 'socialist democracy',[9] 'the critical' approach to participation which will be discussed in Chapter 3, for example, with reference to the Guigliano health project.

The concept of 'community', itself, represents a parallel example of a concept which has been the site of struggle both in terms of its definition, and in terms of its operationalisation within social policies. 'Community' has, after all, been used by the founding fathers of sociology such as Comte in the context of appeals to the social values of pre-capitalist social formations, and by Durkheim, for example, in terms of the development of forms of social cohesion appropriate to the requirements of capitalist rather than pre-capitalist societies. Alternatively the concept of 'community' has figured in the more recent context of liberal/ pluralist, libertarian and socialist usages. And the 'community' of interest, to which the term has been applied, ranges from that of the entire social spectrum, to that of particular social strata, of a sense of community based upon geography, ethnicity, gender or social class, or some combination of these or other interests. More recently too, the term 'community' has been applied to combinations which represent potential alliances, relying upon, but not identical with, class-based definitions and interests (for example in discussions of 'community' politics aimed at developing a politically radical alliance between the traditional working class and other strata, whether these are white-collar workers or the unwaged, women, young people and the elderly).[10]

Alternative definitions of 'community' offer historical parallels, too, in tracing the wider themes of the preceding chapter: the challenge to traditional definitions and approaches (the challenge offered by Marx's analysis to the vision of 'community' offered by more traditionalist theorists such as Comte), a challenge which was followed, too, by a process of reformulation, and retrenchment, but by no means a simple reversal to the preceding ideological/ theoretical status quo.

Similarly problematic and contested, the concepts of 'self-help' and 'self-reliance' have been associated with the legacy of Samuel Smiles, in terms of an individualist/laissez-faire perspective. 'Self-help' has been used in just such a context, in the policy discussions of the Conservative Party, for example, as part of the justification for increasing privatisation within the welfare state. And once again, self-help and self-reliance have been taken up as slogans by governments with goals and perspectives of a fundamentally different character. This has been the case, particularly in the Third World (Tanzania is a case in point) where the basis for the development of public services is very different. The relevance of Third World approaches to these debates (a point discussed later in this chapter and beyond) is crucial both in its own right and in relation to metropolitan black resistance.

Self-help and self-reliance have been particularly attractive concepts, too, for libertarians, whether for the Third World or for the metropolitan situation.[11] For libertarians, the promotion of self-help, as contrasted with publicly financed and bureaucratically organised services, has been central to the evaluation of community initiatives.

More generally, this negative orientation towards the state and all its works is, itself, a further example of the meeting and the blurring of alternative and essentially conflicting perspectives. Anti-statism has, after all, been a central tenet of the individualist/laissez-faire approach, both historically, and specifically within contemporary monetarist approaches. This is not, of course, to suggest that either Thatcherism or Reaganism is actually geared towards the 'withering away' of the state, but rather that the balance between public and private services is intended to be decisively altered, with the former more directly and overtly constrained by the operations and interests of the latter.[12]

At the other end of the political spectrum anti-statism has been part of a mood not only amongst libertarians, but more widely within Marxist debates. Part of the explanation for this could perhaps be traced (as the previous chapter has suggested) in terms of the backgrounds and political experiences of the former student radicals of the late sixties and their white-collar successors in the seventies – the legacy of the ideological influences of libertarian socialist traditions, together with the contradictory experiences of working within official bureaucracies, delivering 'services' such as public housing which the clients, all too often, experience as oppressive and alienating.[13]

Structuralist approaches, which were more influential amongst Marxists in the early seventies, were taken to reinforce this anti-statism, too, emphasising, as they did, the functions for capitalism of the ideological as well as the repressive apparatuses of the state, the education system and the family, for example, the welfare state altogether, in fact, as well as the police and the army, the more traditional foci for analysing the links between the state in its repressive functions and the interests of the status quo.[14]

By the late seventies anti-statism had come to be seen as relatively unproblematic amongst a wide section of radical community workers and activists, a central tenet, almost, part of a mood. But, as it will be suggested subsequently, this anti-statism has not in fact proved to be adequate either as a basis from which to grapple with the challenge from the anti-statism of monetarists, or as a basis from which to develop working alliances within the framework of the formal and rapidly changing political process.

Yet attitudes towards the state, whether the national or the local state, have been particularly central to the practice of community work. Whether directly or indirectly, so much of the focus of both community action and community development has been upon the state as the provider of inappropriate or oppressive services, or, more typically, as the non-provider of sufficient and/or suitable services in response to collective and individual expressions of need (campaigns for public housing repairs, for example, as contrasted with campaigns against urban renewal, especially before the burst of the property boom in 1973).[15] So much community work has, in any case, been funded and ultimately regulated by the state in some form or another. So the concept of the state has been central to the practice of community work, and, once again, this concept has been potentially if not necessarily consistently overtly problematic.

How, then, have community workers and activists been responding to the problematic nature of the conceptual tools of the community work trade? On the one hand, amongst community workers there have been positive responses to the underlying ambiguity of certain key concepts such as these, and the associated blurring of theoretical and political perspectives. Ambiguity represents, after all, some potential space for manoeuvre. If certain concepts can remain apparently neutral, perhaps they can also provide cover for a range of operational strategies, some at least of which would cease to be acceptable to the sponsoring bodies were they to be more clearly defined and/or more overtly expressed.

In a sphere of work which, as a paid activity at any rate, has been relatively underdeveloped, and, in this country, ill-defined and misunderstood, such an approach to community work has possessed, after all, a certain logic. But, as it will be suggested later, one interpretation of the history of public community intervention programmes both in Britain and more widely (e.g., in N. America) has been precisely the narrowing down of these areas of ambiguity and scope for manoeuvre. Some lessons were learnt after all from the US War on Poverty in the sixties; for instance, it showed that Model Cities and other subsequent programmes certainly did not offer such wide-open formulas as 'maximum feasible participation'.

On the contrary it will be suggested that, in face of ideological and political polarisation such as has been occurring in contemporary Britain, such attempts to recover the middle-ground in community work through the use of apparently neutral and neutering definitions and formulas run the risk of reducing community work to the lowest common denominator – and probably at the rightwards end of the middle-ground of the political spectrum – thus losing its appeal for either of the more sharply defined positions.

One alternative approach to the potential battle of ideas around the key concepts of community work has been to resort to a form of abstentionism. If a concept is used in a particular way, or within a particular set of policies, then amongst those who have disagreed, there has been flight as well as fight-back. The concept of 'participation', for example, was discussed in such a context in the late sixties: i.e., if the state developed 'participation strategies' to incorporate protest, then the notion of 'participation', itself, would have to be abandoned by its critics. In parallel, when the notion of resource centres appeared to have perhaps collected some radical connotations there were those who were arguing (for a variety of different reasons) that the term itself should be abandoned. Abstentionism as a strategic response has not been confined, then, to the proponents of any particular theoretical or political position.

Whatever the tactical arguments for abandoning specific concepts and terms, in any particular context, however, abstentionism has serious limitations, too, as a longer-term strategy. Where, after all, does it stop? Ultimately, who is most likely to give up which definitional struggles first?

But what are the alternatives to such a retreat from the key concepts of community work, whether this retreat takes the form of abstentionism, neutering, or the search for the lowest common denominator? How can the development of the past decade or so be built upon theoretically, in such a way as to advance the critical analysis of the assumptions, goals and policies of individualist and pluralist perspectives as well as of the current limitations and ultimate potential for radical alternatives? And how can these essential conflicts be clarified, while allowing space for the development of alliances in practice, spanning some of these theoretical boundaries, at least in relation to immediate, short-term goals, such as the defence and extension of more responsive public services, goals which are typically shared by left pluralists as well as Marxists; in other words, the development of a broadly based, democratic and non-sectarian practice for community work?

While the remaining part of this chapter focuses upon certain key aspects of debates within community work since the late sixties (locating these, where relevant, within the wider theoretical and political debates), the ultimate purpose is the analysis of the potential for alternative and progressive strategies and practices for community work and community action in the eighties.[16]

But before attempting to consider these latter questions, there remains the implicit and prior question of how far such a broad characterisation of recent and contemporary community work debates can, in any case, be sustained.

Alternative approaches

'CDP: community work or class politics' by Corkey and Craig[17] provides an example of the types of critical challenges which were associated with the development of critical practice, from the end of the sixties, especially in relation to the interproject work based upon the experiences of the CDPs (although the article was not actually written until the mid seventies). The first section of this article reviews the community work literature since the 1930s in terms of common underlying assumptions about the nature of society, and of the role of individuals within it. Broadly, the article identifies two distinct theoretical trends. The first is categorised as a view of society and the individual based upon 'high Tory values of individualism, self-help or initiative, which enable the individual to compete in society'. Community work has been perceived, according to such an approach, in terms of its potential for assisting the development of the maturity of individuals through their involvement in group activities, especially self-help activities (the article quotes, for example, 'Developing maturity', a chapter in Batten and Batten).[18] There is, the article concludes, 'no clearer statement than this of the basis of community work theory, i.e. that the inadequacy of individuals is the key and that community work can assist such individuals to mature, and to adapt their way of life to the changes they accept or have had imposed upon them.'

Ultimately community work of this school is concerned with the maintenance of social order and cohesion through the involvement and adaptation of individuals, via the community development process – the achievement of 'community integration'.

Associated with such a view is the stimulus to self-help initiatives 'problem-solving at local level', so that social needs may be met as far as possible through local voluntary effort rather than through the bureaucratic intervention of the state – self-fulfilment via self-help in meeting social needs. Participation is seen as a goal both in its own right – 'making (pluralist) democracy work' – and in terms of its potential for social integration, and the development of more effective information feedback mechanisms.

The second theoretical trend which the article identifies is associated with pluralist perspectives. Pluralist perspectives have had, in general, a key influence upon debates within and around the welfare state, certainly since the late nineteenth and early twentieth centuries (the empirical work of Booth and the critique which the Webbs offered of the Poor Law could, for example, be categorised in such terms). In this article, the influences of pluralist approaches to community development, however, are discussed in particular relation to more recent concerns, including the initiatives developed by three publications associated with the Calouste Gulbenkian Foundation. (It should be noted that the Calouste Foundation has in practice also funded other approaches to community action.) The first, *Community Work*, by Leaper,[19] adopts definitions which emphasise participation within the structure of existing (pluralist) capitalist institutions. The Calouste Gulbenkian Foundation's Community Work Group similarly roots community work within the framework of the prevalent values of Western capitalist democracies, including both an emphasis on the individual, and upon participation, to enable the powerless to join in the political process or, in other words, to compete within the existing rules of the game. The sources of the political powerlessness of the poor remain unexamined in such an analysis, rejecting, as it does, the notion that political powerlessness is determined, in turn, by wider structures of inequality rooted in the very structure of the predominant form of economic relations.

Typically, pluralist approaches to participation would seem to rest upon an underemphasis of the essentially problematic nature of the concept of 'need'. Even if individuals and/or communities may require some stimulus and information inputs, via the community development process, to set the participation exercise in motion, ultimately the people are assumed to be in the best position to know what they want, to understand their own needs better than outside professionals and agencies, however well intentioned.

Some of the limitations to such an apparently attractive but essentially populist assumption are discussed later in this chapter, and in relation to specific issues, such as health in Chapter 3 (populist, spontaneous demands around health being typically to defend high-technology, curative medicine, for instance, rather than for a healthier living and working environment (or even for the more individual solutions of jogging and bran). Pluralist approaches, while recognising certain of these issues, in practice, typically resist analyses of the limitations of spontaneity, which confront the issues of consciousness in terms of its roots in the structure of capitalist society, and of the reproduction of a hegemonic bourgeois ideology, so pluralist approaches usually fail to confront the tendency of the working class and its allies to perceive their situation, interests and needs within the framework and the limitations of the status quo, rather than to see the potential for any fundamentally different alternative.

In summary, the Calouste Gulbenkian Foundation publications are taken to typify the prevailing, pluralist perspectives in the teaching, sponsorship and practice of community work in the early and mid-seventies. As Lambert noted in an essay in the same collection, this was, after all, 'the most common and widely accepted account ... the dominant view of the period, in community work, as in discussions of the Welfare State more generally.'[20]

Pluralist perspectives, in fact, covered a broad range of styles. In addition to the mainstream of the community work 'profession', for example, the particular approach to community action (to develop 'community politics'), adopted initially by the Young

Liberals, represented a different style even if an essentially parallel strategy. Ultimately, then Corkey and Craig characterised 'community politics' as 'simply another name for raising local demands about local issues, a technique used by the full range of political interests, whether or not they related the development of such locally based alliances to the momentum of class politics.'

At this point, it should be emphasised that alternative approaches based upon the recognition of the centrality of class divisions do *not*, by definition, imply any wholesale rejection of the development of alliances, including alliances which span class divisions. Even radical campaigns to support public transport, such as the Fares Fair Campaign in the GLC area in 1982, have clearly enjoyed the backing of a broad alliance of interests. The point being made is specifically *not* that alternative approaches to community work and action necessitate a sectarian practice, but that, as Corkey and Craig argue, they do involve *selectivity* about the development of such alliances based upon a class analysis which places the interests of working people at the core.

However self-evident this may seem, the point requires emphasis, not least because of the nature of the attacks on the Corkey and Craig article and the implication that alternative approaches to community work based upon a Marxist analysis can represent a fundamental rejection of alliances, even a rejection of locally based community work altogether.[21] In fact, the article by Corkey and Craig goes on to outline precisely such a strategy for developing alliances, both locally and nationally, rooted in a class-based analysis while reflecting local aspirations and needs.

This analysis starts from the assumption that the problems which are experienced by working people in the 'community' are related not simply to relative poverty, both individually and in terms of their immediate environment, or even to their political powerlessness, but rather that these are all aspects of a structure of inequality which is rooted in the dominant form of economic relations, the capitalist mode of production, based upon a fundamental conflict of interests between the owners of capital and the working class. From such an analysis, it follows, Corkey and Craig argue, that it is the collective efforts of working people that play the key role in progressive social change.

This recognition of the limitations of spontaneity (and the

consequent necessity for confronting the class biases inherent in the pluralist politics of supposedly 'neutral' community participation exercises) had a longer history, too, emerging in the programmes of certain of the community workshops, in the early seventies. Cowley, for example, rejected any notion that community organisers should simply act as supports to 'whatever struggles are surfacing', in favour of an approach based upon critical dialogue. Pluralist approaches to community work, Cowley argues, typically 'write off those organisers who go too far in raising hard political issues' as manipulators and thus as exploiters of their client communities. In contrast Cowley argues that:[22]

> In a class-ridden society, where the dice are loaded against the working class on every count, the Workshop [Camden Community Workshop] makes no pretence to this so-called 'neutrality' of the respectable community worker. Neutrality, in such a situation, could be nothing more than effective collusion with those forces which have an interest in maintaining the status quo, collusion with the respectable manipulators, that is.

Yet the implications of such an approach were by no means to neglect, let alone to deny, the significance of spontaneous expressions of 'felt need' as starting points for community action; the workshop's strategy 'depends on taking "felt needs" in terms of locally experienced problems seriously, working from the concrete issue and achieving whatever intermediate goals we can'.[23] But the Camden Community Workshop did differentiate itself from pluralist approaches by its insistence upon the necessity for creating a critical dialogue around these felt needs, and for locating these community struggles within a longer term and alternative strategy.

Community work based upon such an analysis, then, relates its longer-term aims and objectives to the developing political struggles of the movement including the movement's necessary self-confidence and self-consciousness in rejecting capitalist ideology and definitions of 'needs' more specifically, in favour of an alternative, collectively based and specifically socialist ideology and strategic programme.

Corkey and Craig go on to offer examples of such forms of

practice, within the structure of the state/Home Office's own Community Development Project, based as it was upon a fundamentally different analysis. Examples included housing campaigns and employment work, aimed particularly at building the links between community groups and the trade union movement. The authors conclude that underlying the CDP interproject reports is a 'bottom up' strategy to support working-class actions in defence of their class interests, and to develop effective challenges to the operations of private capital.

Subsequent chapters will focus more specifically upon the implications of such an alternative strategic approach to community work in relation to employment and housing, for example. While this approach is contrasted with that of more conventional approaches, based upon individualistic and pluralistic perspectives, it should nevertheless be emphasised that, in practice, in relation to short-term demands at least, these differences may be far less clearly distinguishable, even temporarily submerged, within any particular broadly based campaign. This question has represented a recurrent theme, relating as it does to the issue of incorporation, the process of the reabsorption of working-class demands for intermediate goals, supported by both pluralists and Marxists.

Gortz, for example, writing at the end of the sixties, concluded that however advanced the demands of community action movements around issues of collective consumption, if they remained spontaneous, without a longer-term overall political perspective (i.e., self-consciously socialist), they risked being 'reabsorbed by capitalism; the end result would be in a "mixed economy" of the Scandinavian type, in which the power of capital and alienated labour survive while "welfare" is given to all.'[24]

Translated into the British context, state initiatives to promote citizen participation and community development were considered in terms of their capacity to re-establish social integration to head off the prospects for public disorder based upon ethnic minority grievances and 'to buy off' the escalating demands of the working-class clientele of the welfare state. The history of community development has been traced in similar terms, i.e., of state policies to promote or to re-establish social and political integration whether in colonial situations (the British in Africa, India and Malaya, for example) or amongst socially deprived metropolitan populations (the US War on Poverty and the UK CDPs, for example).[25]

Such programmes were attractive, it was argued, because they represented relatively minor public investment, while at the same time stimulating self-help activities to lessen the burden of further escalating demands for public services, and additionally developing more effective feedback mechanisms to increase the efficiency of the expanding official bureaucracies in central (and particularly at this period) local government.[26]

Such recurrent emphasis upon the co-optive and potentially repressive aspects of community work fits into a context of 'coming to terms' with one's discipline and/or profession (the set of studies called 'Course Counter-Course Critiques', for example, were part of this trend) – a focus upon questioning the accepted 'givens' of the preceding period up to the latter part of the sixties. Any assumption that even apparently pluralist community development and public participation programmes were essentially 'radical' was challenged as part of this wider questioning process amongst radicals in general and professionals in relation to their own specific work situation.

Later in the seventies, the women's movement took this process further by questioning the potential of the welfare state in general, and of community work in particular, for reinforcing the institutionalisation of gender differentiation as well as that of social class.[27]

In fact – and in view of subsequent responses, this has to be emphasised – these critics were by no means rejecting the notion that community action possessed any genuinely radical potential, nor even that the young professionals in expanding and increasingly routinised public service sector occupations such as community work could play any creative role in developing a critical practice.

For example, in the article in *Radical Social Work*, Mayo concluded that, having stressed the limitations and indeed the repressive aspects of community work, it was essential to identify the potential for community organising both in terms of defensive struggles and within a wider and longer-term movement for radical social change. So, we were not rejecting community work or denying its relevance to the wider movement; but there was, all the same, an important problem of emphasis with this type of analysis. In summary, this related to an over-reliance upon structuralist approaches to Marxism including the work of Althusser, Poulantzas and Castells, emphasising as they did the functions of social institutions for capitalism, including the overtly less repressive and more benign institutions of the welfare state. These were analysed in terms of their functions for reproducing a trained, healthy and contented labour force, fully socialised into capitalist forms of social relations. There were also reservations, of course, expressed even at that time and incorporated into some of our debates, but these received, typically, less emphasis.

Since then (the mid seventies), structuralism has been subjected to critiques from a range of different theoretical stances. The 1978 conference on Urban Change and Conflict, for example, expressed a reaction against the 'new departures' of the structuralists, which had been presented in the previous annual conference by Castells himself.[28] Structuralism had become out of vogue by the end of the seventies. In terms of the debates about the welfare state and community action, urban conflict and the political potential of 'urban social movements' (Castells's own terminology) the specific critiques of earlier structuralist approaches focused upon the following major areas: 1) the over-emphasis upon functionalist explanations in general and upon social reproduction as opposed to production, in particular; 2) the excessive concern with the relatively autonomous interventions of the state in relation to the former, rather than the latter sphere; 3) the ambiguity and inadequacy of the notions of collective consumption and indeed of urban social movements; and 4) the over-formalistic theoretical model which under-emphasised the relationship between the development of theory and of empirical studies.

In fact Althusser's own focus upon the functions which are performed for the interests of capital not just by the repressive arms of the state (such as the police and army), but by a range of institutions including those of the welfare state (such as the education system) had been part of his wider concern to re-establish the centrality of Marxist concepts. *Reading Capital*,[29] for example, was part of an attempt to counter a set of looser usages, imbued with the humanistic and libertarian ideologies which had been current within the student movement and its aftermath at the end of the sixties. In practice, however, an over-emphasis upon the functions of the welfare state could actually be taken over to justify precisely such (libertarian) anti-statist approaches. Community struggles could then be posed as being simplistically *against* rather than over and around the institutions of the welfare state.

Although this was not actually the position which was argued, for example, by *In and Against the State*,[30] such an approach did enjoy a certain currency, at least until the Labour government's cuts of the mid seventies were given a new impetus and direction by the election of the Thatcher government (1979) and even afterwards; for instance the publication of such articles as 'The sale of council houses: does it matter?',[31] questioning the need to defend public housing from privatisation. Leonard,[32] for example, found it necessary to confront such positions, and to discuss their inherent limitations, as part of the discussion of left alternatives to monetarism, in relation to the welfare state. *Community Action* magazine, similarly, in its 50th issue focused upon the apparent contradictions involved in defending the bureaucratic and indeed repressive institutions of the welfare state.

In the very first days of the new Tory government in 1979 there were even expressions of disbelief about the nature of the monetarists' attack. The ultimate logic of an extreme functionalist perspective would, after all, be to suggest that if the welfare state is so uniquely suited to guaranteeing social reproduction in the contemporary capitalist state, then whatever the laissez-faire/monetarist rhetoric, the underlying structure of welfare would remain inviolate.

In fact, of course, the critics of the earlier structuralists had already pointed out the major flaws of such a position, the over-emphasis upon the role of the state in terms of social reproduction as opposed to production, and the structuralists' relative inattention to concrete empirical analyses which could take account of how far particular outcomes for welfare are affected by the specific effects of time and space, and in relation to class struggles.[33] And as soon as the role of the state in relation to production is re-emphasised the real interests of a monetarist government, not in abolishing so much as restructuring and increasingly privatising welfare provision, become more immediately comprehensible.[34]

Certain of the structuralists, themselves, have shifted their focus in any case. Castells, for example, in the study of Dunkerque, went some way towards meeting both types of criticisms, with his concern to focus upon production and to develop his formal model by means of a case study.

In summary, structuralist approaches to the 'urban question' and the scenario for community action within a wider socialist movement have been drawn in two opposing directions. On the one hand, there have been reformulations which have taken the discussion forward by bringing it back closer to more 'classical' Marxist approaches, re-emphasising the primacy of the sphere of production. This is linked with the need for more concrete analysis of the potential for progressive struggles around state welfare provision, relating the often relatively fragmented community struggles around urban planning issues, 'urban social movements', to the mainstream of radical politics, whether within the trade union movement, broad social movements such as the women's movement and the peace movement, or direct political struggles (e.g., within the Labour Party).

This theme of the need to develop alliances between community struggles/urban social movements and progressive politics has been a key theme, not only in relation to the theoretical attempts to move beyond structuralist Marxism, but within the mainstream of radical writing and practice (from Ken Coates's and R. Silburn's conclusions on community struggles in Nottingham[35] through the CDP interproject reports, the Corkey and Craig article itself, and more recent discussions, for example, on the potential for joint community and trade union struggles around employment issues[36]).

Alternatively, the attempt to move beyond the limitations of structuralist approaches has been associated, too, with moves away from Marxism altogether, both in general terms and in relation to the urban question and community action more specifically.

Before moving on to consider the revival of the radical right and of rightwards shifts within the pluralist perspective in relation to community work and community action from the latter part of the seventies, it is worth noting that pluralist critiques, of Castells, for example, were by no means simply confined to attempts to refute either structuralism in particular or even Marxism more generally. Saunders,[37] for example, while clearly not a Marxist, draws upon Marxist insights and raises questions, in turn, particularly about the potential for an effective radical basis for 'urban social movements' which are directly relevant for Marxists. So Saunders emphasises, for instance, the blurring of class distinctions around issues of social reproduction; council housing, for example, has been taken to represent *the* working-class tenure, whereas in the South East of England, in particular, owner-occupation is of course a significant working-class housing form, too.

While in practice, community action on housing estates in working-class localities in many parts of Britain may indeed be readily identifiable, if by no means identical with working-class politics more generally, this may not be so self-evidently the case in less socially homogenous areas, such as much of Inner London. Here, community politics may be less typically reducible to class politics, particularly on issues such as education, health and transport which may be less obviously class-specific than such issues as council housing repairs.

The challenge posed by the Marxists has also led to approaches, which, while acknowledging their debt, move on to develop counter-arguments and strategies. So, in relation to debates about the inner city, for example, Kennett and Hall[38] recognise the insights of Massey and Meegan[39] into the industrial rationalisation process and its differential spacial impacts, together with the relevance of Marxist critiques more generally. Yet Kennett and Hall go on to discuss policy solutions which are fundamentally in contrast: they emphasise the case for encouraging the small firm, for example, and the informal economy, which could, Hall suggests, be assisted by a relaxation of planning, health and safety and employment protection legislation – in other words the concept of the 'enterprise zone', based upon a supposed revival of individualist/laissez-faire approaches. In this, then, they come closer to the responses of the radical right, with their emphasis upon freeing the market mechanisms from the constraints of state intervention.

The increasing emphasis upon the importance of jobs in relation to community work has had similar ambiguities. In an earlier period, in the seventies, raising the jobs question – the 'local economy' – in this context was most typically associated with Marxist approaches (CDP publications for example).[40] Since then, the jobs question has been taken up in a variety of ways, including policy initiatives to promote private investment, such as those developed by the minister in response to the Toxteth 'riots' in Liverpool in 1981, a blend of monetarist and more reformist goals and strategies.

Overall, without in any sense underestimating the challenge of the radical right (as outlined, for example, in relation to social policy[41]), the 'community' policies of the Thatcher government would not seem to have been originally, uniquely and unambiguously hostile. Relatively liberal Tories have been writing within the broadly pluralist framework more characteristic of the previous decade. Linda Chalker, for example, has made the case for the relevance of supporting voluntary effort and self-help through community work initiatives, to the point of allowing some space for frictions, and even conflicts, between community groups and service providers.[42] At another, and of course more distant, and thus perhaps more comfortable level, Conservative MPs have been prepared to support the case for the continuation of community initiatives via the EEC anti-poverty programme (discussed in more detail in Chapter 3).

Rather than major condemnations of past community initiatives and strategies, the response has been, more typically, to support developments which emphasise self-help and voluntary effort, and which exclude any more overtly challenging, let alone political, scope for community work. 'Community Chest' type schemes were to be piloted, for example, to draw in private sector funding in support of self-help initiatives.

Similarly, the urban programme and partnership schemes survived their initial scrutinies albeit with tighter definitions. With the partnership schemes, for example, the views of chambers of commerce have to be taken into account in relation to jobs schemes (which are to be prioritised) to ensure that the interests of the private sector are safeguarded. The voluntary sector is to be encouraged especially in innovative and cost-*effective* projects to meet social need. Meanwhile projects run by community groups, themselves, are to be subject to specific ministerial scrutiny: 'Projects must be seen to be *politically neutral* and should not be used for party political propaganda. Projects which show a party political bias or would involve *political propaganda* will not therefore be approved for grant aid.'[43]

On occasion, the Conservative government has even given

legislative support to participation schemes (the Tenants' Charter) when these have fitted readily into a packge of restructuring and privatisation – in this case, the sale of council housing.[44]

To summarise, initially anyway the main thrust of Conservative policies towards community work and community participation schemes has been not to abolish them, but to restructure them, to neutralise them or even to tie them more closely to the operations of the private market and to build them into the structures of an increasingly privatised welfare state.

An alternative response (as it has already been suggested) has been to attempt to recapture the middle-ground; presenting accounts and justifications for publicly sponsored community initiatives, in terms which, whether or not this is the intention of their authors, can be considered acceptable, even to the new right, in fact. Broadly two strands are identifiable in this process, accounts which emphasise the significance of essentially ambiguous concepts (including the concept of community itself, of course, together with concepts such as self-help and self-reliance), which can then be interpreted by others in varying ways, and accounts which minimise the political elements within community development, and concentrate instead upon community work as a more neutral and technical exercise. Both strands tend to be located within a pluralist theoretical framework, which verges closer, on occasion, to the ideological framework of laissez-faire (and in the cases of certain authors, explicitly to the politics of the SDP). The promotion of self-help in welfare via the voluntary sector is compared, by Hatch, for example, in some senses at least, with the 'emergence of a self-service economy',[45] based upon the notions of Gershuny.[46]

Hatch locates his interest in the voluntary sector (following the Wolfenden Committee Report) in relation to the alienating bureaucracies of the welfare state, as well as in terms of the pressures to find cheaper alternative forms of welfare provision based upon self-help. Beveridge's *Voluntary Action* is taken as a reference point:[47]

in a totalitarian society all action outside the citizen's home, and it may be much that goes on there, is directed and controlled by the State. By contrast, the vigour and abundance of Voluntary Action, outside one's home, individually and in association with other citizens, for bettering one's own life and that of one's fellows, are the distinguishing marks of a free society.

Hatch goes on to discuss 'participation' and 'involvement' programmes in the seventies, in relation to Beveridge's view of the value of voluntary action as an essential element in a plural society imbued with the spirit of mutual aid and philanthrophy.

Community intervention programmes, then, acquire a third justification. In addition to the value of promoting self-help, as a cheaper alternative to statutory services, and as a means of ensuring flexibility to counteract the bureaucracy of official structures, voluntary action is to be supported more widely as an essential plank of pluralist democracy.

The collection of essays edited by Hadley and McGrath include similar comments about the value of participation and voluntary effort. For example Jones starts from the position that 'the devolution of responsibility is a good to pursue. . . . For me it is an essential part of democracy.'[48] The theme of the collection, more generally, centres around the issue of the decentralisation of services via the 'patch system' and the fusion of statutory work with voluntary action in the community, to maximise local involvement and, of course, community-based self-help initiatives.

Similar themes emerge in Hadley and Hatch.[49] Conventional left demands for the extension of democratic control are dismissed as effectively entailing party or trade union control. Left and right together, then, are both branded as benevolent paternalists, or even *petits fonctionnaires* with direct personal interests in the expansion of *étatisme*. The 'new radicalism', which is posed by the authors as the alternative, consists, then, of a revitalisation of the middle pluralist ground around decentralisation/'small is beautiful' and the promotion of the voluntary sector, within a wider pluralist framework of redistributive policies.

Some of the implications of such an approach in the current political climate, particularly the emphasis upon self-help and community care, have already been spelt out elsewhere.[50] Clearly, there have been aspects which have attracted the interest of the Thatcher government; and clearly, too, the main thrust of Conservative initiatives in the voluntary sector has been compatible with such a line of argument, especially in view of the ambiguity of so many of the key concepts. The promotion of self-help, for example, within the framework of redistributive social policies (as advocated by the pluralists) is not, after all, the equivalent of self-help, as a substitute for such policies. Yet, in the debates around the Barclay Report, for example, an emphasis upon supporting self-help, voluntary effort and community-based initiatives has been located at the more progressive end of the spectrum.

It has not, in any case, been suggested that the 'new pluralist radicalism' has been consciously promoted by its authors, in terms which would blur the distinctions between pluralist and individualist/laissez-faire/monetarist perspectives, in order to make their policy proposals politically acceptable to the present government. On the contrary, the point of emphasising these aspects is merely to indicate some of the potential and actual outcomes – which is, of course, quite a different matter.

The second type of approach to the recovery of the middle-ground, and the re-establishment of the legitimacy of community work within a pluralist or even not so pluralist democracy has focused, as it has already been suggested, upon its more technical and overtly neutral aspects. *Skills in Neighbourhood Work*[51] and the introduction to *The Boundaries of Change in Community Work*[52] would both seem to provide illustrations of such a project within the pluralist perspective. *Skills in Neighbourhood Work*, for example, starts explicitly from the view that community work is under attack, and that unless the skills and practice of community work are made explicit and developed more vigor-ously, then society will 'lose interest in, or turn against, a form of community intervention which is inadequately described, analysed and evaluated'.

Henderson and Thomas accept that in some senses their work is influenced by the challenge offered by structuralist/Marxist arguments, and the need to answer these with a more modest set of claims for the political potential of community, and with renewed justifications for neighbourhood work of a less overtly political nature. Similarly, the introduction to *The Boundaries of Change in Community Work* emphasises the organisational rather than the political achievements of community workers, and their skills in equilibration between the various individuals, groups and organisations that make demands upon them.

In fact Henderson's, Jones's and Thomas's view of community work as a relatively marginal activity has not been in question per se (since Marxist approaches have not, in any case, by definition, accorded a central but a secondary role to locally based and typically consumption-focused struggles). Similarly the relevance of developing practice skills and techniques is not in itself in question. The key differences have centred rather upon the authors' reticence in accepting the relevance of alternative theoretical perspectives (or 'value sets', in their terminology) to community work practice, their favoured form seeming to be some combination of professional and pluralist values.

As it has already been suggested, such an approach was indeed broadly accepted until the mid to late sixties. Since then, it has been challenged from both the left and from the right.

How far, then, can the pluralist middle-ground be recaptured, and in whose interest would this be, in the current political and socio-economic climate? The answer to both questions depends in part upon the analysis of the nature of the challenges to community work. In particular, if community work's very survival is at stake, then the recovery of the middle-ground would seem to have certain attractions as a strategy. In fact, however, it has been suggested here, that the monetarists are not necessarily bent upon attacking community work's continued existence (nor indeed are Marxists, of course), despite the caricature to that effect that has been prevalent in some of the pluralist literature.

But if the attack from the right is more in the nature of a restructuring and redefinition of community work's goals and appropriate spheres of operation, re-emphasising the relevance of self-help, for example, together with the potential contribution of the private sector, then the middle-ground is both sensitive and problematic. In such a climate, the defence of community work in relatively neutral, technical and a-political terms can be used to justify precisely such a restructuring process. One of the further possible implications of such a potentially rightwards shift within the pluralist sphere could be, then, to rule out some of the most stimulating community development policy moves, within left Labour councils, for example, as beyond the pale of professional community work.

Current responses in relation to the possibility of developing a radical and non-sectarian practice

Meanwhile, what has been the response of the left in reply to these reactions to the challenge of Marxist approaches, over the seventies, including the re-emergence of the radical right, and the attempts at the recovery of the middle-ground within the pluralist spectrum?

Firstly, with increasing pressure from cuts, and from strategies for restructuring, more generally, there has been considerable emphasis upon the case for democratising the welfare state. This theme comes to the fore, for example, in *Towards Socialist Welfare Work*,[53] where 'democratic reconstruction' – an increased and extended democracy – is posed as the key issue for a socialist strategy for welfare. In fact, the systematic exclusion from this process (of democratic involvement) has, the authors argue, been responsible for laying the welfare state open for the attack from the right. Similar views have been current more widely amongst radical community and social workers, teachers and students at the beginning of the eighties. At the first Critical Social Policy Conference, in London in 1980, for example, there was considerable emphasis upon the failures of the welfare state to involve its own clientele, so that working-class people were too alienated to bother to defend these bureaucratic structures from the attack of the radical right.

In fact, as it has been argued elsewhere,[54] systematic evidence to support such a view has not (at least yet) been forthcoming. Certainly community-based struggles to resist 'the cuts' have been problematic, but so, in such a climate, have been workplace campaigns to resist redundancies and factory closures. Whether or not particular groups of clients have turned against the welfare state because of its alienating bureaucratic procedures, certain aspects, at least, such as the NHS and education have been consistently popular in opinion polls (even with all their inherent limitations; there are other studies which illustrate the still high level of satisfaction and the often depressingly low expectations of the clients of the health service, in particular). The move towards private medical insurance/private education could certainly be explained just as plausibly in terms of disaffection with the effects of the cuts themselves, the scarcity rather than the repressive nature of state involvement. This is certainly *not* to argue that all was well with the services as they were, of course. All that is being suggested is that on the whole, most people prefer even their local hospital or school to the alternative of none at all.

It has been suggested that for a considerable proportion of working people, 'most of their time and/or energy, is spent in surviving from day to day, *not* as protagonists nor yet antagonists of the welfare state . . . .' This was certainly the view of one of the tenant activists involved in the South Wales Association of Tenants, discussed in Chapter 6. To propose democratisation as a solution to their problems, then, is to misunderstand their situation quite fundamentally, and to imply a present level of involvement and concern way beyond that which their actual situation warrants.

Finally, calls for democratisation have to take account of the practical tasks involved in developing the organisational basis for effective participatory structures. As Chapter 3 considers in more detail, for example, the involvement of community groups in the management structures of their local area resource centres proved to be typically problematic. 'Democracy' had to be built up and developed, not taken as given.

This is, of course, in no sense to imply that the democratisation of the welfare state ought not to be a goal, merely to emphasise its essentially problematic character. Demands for democratisation have to be set in the context of the arguments, for example (as it has been suggested earlier in this chapter), about the nature of spontaneous 'felt needs', which tend to reflect dominant values and interests (patients' demands for drugs and injections) and that pluralist participation strategies per se offer no effective challenge to the structure of bias within the political structures of capitalist society. Democratisation campaigns, for example, within the Labour Party and the trade union movement have certainly been associated with strategies to develop the constituency for more progressive policies but these campaigns have to be set within the context of the 'critical dialogue' to win support for alternative policies rather than assuming any automatic, inherent rank and file support for progressive policies. Hindess, for example, has discussed the fallacy of assuming that there is a groundswell of popular support for left policies within the Labour Party, simply waiting to be unleashed as a result of the introduction of more democratic procedures.[55] On the contrary, given the widespread acceptance of the framework of the dominant ideology, Marxists would not expect democratisation, or even moves for direct as opposed to representative democratisation, to be unproblematic as a strategy for socialism. Without this perspective, calls for democratisation per se risk merely fuelling the anti-statism characteristic not only of the libertarian left, but of the radical right.

In fact, the limitations of simplistic appeals to democratise the welfare state as a solution to the contradictions of recent struggles to defend it have been widely recognised. For example, while emphasising the relevance of community groups' struggles in developing a trade union style consciousness around consumer issues, and in providing experiences of taking a little power that 'will grow into the consciousness that leads to class action', Corrigan and Leonard also emphasise the ultimate necessity for the transformation of community politics into class politics.[56]

As it has already been suggested, the democratisation issue has been taken up, too, as part of attempts to build bridges between the development of progressive politics within the mainstream of the labour movement (the Labour Party and the trade unions) and within community groupings. So while radical professionals and community activists have been facing up to the issue of participation in the formal political process, progressives and radicals within the Labour Party, in particular, have been examining new ways of coming out to meet them and relating to their struggles. Such a process can be traced, for example, in South Yorkshire, West Midlands and Greater London – developments in the latter being discussed in more detail in the final chapter.

So, for example, financial support for community groups has become a major policy issue, with support to be offered on less of a patron-client basis, with the groups taking part too, in dialogues with councillors around the relevant policy areas, more generally (for instance, via meetings of women's groups, law centres and gay organisations). The GLC-sponsored London Assembly, a meeting of some 700 representatives of community and trade union organisations in February 1982, represented an attempt to take this process of developing dialogue further. More local and issue-orientated assemblies are planned on the basis of the recognition of the political autonomy of these assemblies.

In the context of the Tory government's further curtailment of such powers as still remain to local government, such a strategy of going out to win popular support for their policies makes obvious political sense for any local authority which is attempting to develop alternative policies. Such a strategy would seem to rest upon conscious uses of theory too. In particular, the experiences of 'Red Bologna' and the achievements of a communist-controlled municipality within the framework of a series of fundamentally hostile national governments[57] have evidently been a source of interest, together with some of their theoretical underpinnings in the work of Gramsci, for example.

Lebas,[58] for instance, discusses the relevances of Gramsci's concept of the war of position, as contrasted with the war of movement, or in other words, the potential for struggling over and for the state, including struggling for parts of the state, such as municipalities, and developing a new form of politics, culture and consciousness which would then point the way towards the establishment of socialism. Whilst such an approach could be taken to underpin strategies which assume the possibility of an incrementalist path in a socialist direction, Gramsci himself was not, of course, implying, that the war of position necessarily involved a reformist as contrasted with an inherently Marxist-Leninist analysis. The political potential of such a strategy in the shorter term would seem to have key implications in relation to the development of a radical strategy for community work and community development.

The significance of intermediate struggles has emerged, too, in relation to the increasingly significant debates on the left about feminist practice in community work. 'The personal is political', is, after all a powerful slogan in relation to practice and short-term strategies as well as in relation to longer-term goals. The relationship between the development of socialist feminist theory in general, and of feminist perspectives in community work is also a recurrent theme for radical community work in the eighties.

Finally, there would seem to be an identifiable strand involving more conscious attempts to relate the development of radical community development and community work theory and practice in Britain with those elsewhere, including those of the Third World. In the late sixties and early seventies, there was almost an implicit turning away from the experiences of the Third World, associated with the rejection of traditional and typically colonially based approaches to community development (the Batten School, for example). So attempts to shift the focus of the *Community Development Journal*, for example, in a more radical direction, became loosely but erroneously associated with attempts to focus increasingly upon community development within urban situations, in Britain and N. America (or increasingly now, in the EEC). In fact, the special issue of *Community Development Journal* devoted to the Third World starts, quite explicitly, from rejecting such a division between 'developed' and 'under-developed' community development strategies and practice.

A more internationalist focus for community development has been the concern too of the radical charity, War on Want. War on Want in fact initiated a programme of support for community initiatives in the UK as part of a wider programme to win greater understanding of the links between progressive struggles in the Third World and in metropolitan situations, including, in particular, the struggles of oppressed racial minorities. By systematically raising the question of the links between exploitation, racism and oppression at home and abroad, they are, then, potentially building into their work an internationalist educative programme.[59]

This potential for building internationalist perspectives and actual links between projects and even local activists began to emerge, at least embryonically, too, within the context of the EEC anti-poverty programme. Although this aspect of the programme had barely started to develop when the funds were cut off, there were at least the beginnings of creative co-operation, not only between project workers but also between local activists, for example, in an international demonstration in Brussels in support of the continuation of the programme organised in 1981, as the following chapter explains.

3 Community action and anti-poverty programmes

The first section (Chapters 1 and 2) has focused upon the question of community action and publicly sponsored community development and poverty programmes in Britain in relation to wider processes of political change, from the late sixties through to the end of the seventies and beyond. In this second section, we shall be illustrating certain aspects of those processes, and the theoretical debates which were associated with them, through a case study, involving community action elements within the British projects in the European Economic Community's anti-poverty programme.

While these projects, and indeed the entire EEC anti-poverty programme more generally, could be located within the context of the politics of preceding programmes in Britain and North America, whether positively or negatively (the lessons learnt together with the lessons not learnt from the War on Poverty or CDP, for example, discussed previously), there were significant differences too, differences which related, in turn, to the wider changes, discussed in the first section.

The EEC anti-poverty programme itself, and the specific examples of community action within the UK projects which have been included here, illustrate certain aspects of the wider processes of realignment and redefinition (which were discussed in Chapter 2). Within the programme and the projects there were contradictory pressures, on the one hand towards polarisation, and on the other towards the recovery of the pluralist and relatively more consensual 'middle-ground'.

The programme and the projects included, too, illustrations of our other major concern, the development of a practice that is both radical and, at the same time, non-sectarian, a practice which relates to the immediate and locally perceived issues of daily life as well as to the wider structural strategies for progressive social change.

Critics have, in the past, concentrated upon precisely this issue of the correspondence or lack of correspondence between theory and practice in their evaluations of the relevance of emerging radical theoretical perspectives. They have argued, for example, that 'the more radical the ideology, the less correlation there is between it and practice'[1] (i.e., that radical practice has not, at least yet, emerged). Or, alternatively, it has been suggested that, at least amongst the cruder Marxists, radical theories have led to nihilistic and sectarian practices, involving the ultimate rejection of community work if not also community action altogether.[2]

As we have already set out in Chapter 2, one of our major concerns is to examine the possibilities for refuting precisely such criticisms; to relate in fact to the analysis of the potential for community work and community action in the eighties for broadly based and democratic yet radical social change.[3]

Now, clearly these were not the specific goals of the initiators of the European programme. All that is being suggested is that it is possible to trace certain attempts to develop such a practice, within and between various of the ensuing projects both in Britain and elsewhere in the EEC on a cross-national basis. But before attempting the location, analysis and evaluation of such projects the programme itself requires some introduction.

The pilot projects and poverty

The EEC programme to combat poverty was conceptualised by the heads of state of the newly enlarged community in 1972, although this programme was not actually launched for another three years in 1975 (initially for two years, subsequently renewed until the end of 1980).

The purpose of the programme in the words of the Council of Ministers' decision of July 1975 was:

> to test and develop new methods of helping persons beset by or threatened by poverty in the Community.

The definition of poverty which they employed was a relative one:

individuals or families may be considered in general to be in poverty when they have a command of resources so deficient that they are excluded from ordinary living patterns, customs and activities of the Member State in which they live.

The Working Paper published by the commission in June 1974 set down various criteria for the selection of the pilot schemes. These criteria may be summarised as follows: 1) the schemes should be original; in other words designed to 'test new methods'; 2) they should have the potential to be extended into wider programmes in the future; 3) they should include systematic programming, reporting and analysis of the projects' impact; 4) in addition, the schemes should involve the participation of the poor themselves; 5) finally, there was also, running through the early discussions of the poverty programme, some concern to encourage schemes which would deal with problems common to more than one member state, so that the experience gained might be relevant to the formation of policy at Community as well as at national level.

The EEC projects which were eventually operationalised within this programme combined a mixture of research (cross-national studies of poverty, directly sponsored by the commission, including a study of The Perception of Poverty in Europe) and twenty-one pilot projects initially, which were, in the most general sense, all considered as community action projects. In fact, these community action pilot projects fell into three major categories: there were service delivery programmes (including welfare rights and tribunal representation programmes); services for deprived and marginal groups, such as the homeless and gypsies (Ireland); and there were projects which could more accurately be considered as community action projects, including the three UK area resource centres (in London, Govan (Glasgow) and South Wales) which are discussed in more detail subsequently. Before coming on to these resource centres, however, the EEC programme itself, more generally, requires location, in terms of the preceding discussions.

One view[4] explains the heads of states' initiative in 1972 in terms of the need for the EEC to be presented with a more 'human face'; to develop the legitimacy of the EEC, by demonstrating concern with social goals (including the reduction of 'disparities in living conditions') as contrasted with the previous emphasis upon economic goals within the Community, whether these were perceived as the promotion of capitalist accumulation, or more popularly perceived as the accumulation of wine lakes and butter mountains as the result of the Community Agricultural Policy (CAP).

In the early seventies the heads of state discussed the case for the programme in terms of the persistence of poverty within a wider context of affluence (reflecting in fact the ways in which poverty had been re-emerging on national political agendas). As the study of poverty and inequality in Common Market countries edited by George and Lawson[5] has demonstrated, despite economic growth coupled with improved welfare programmes, it was becoming increasingly evident in the late sixties, at national government level, in a range of EEC member states, as well as in Britain itself, that poverty had by no means been abolished. For example, in Belgium, as one commentator has recorded, 'in the late sixties, after twenty-five years of social security and in the midst of welfare, the existence of modern forms of poverty was rediscovered. The point at issue was quite an extensive group of people who had been unable to participate in the general prosperity'.[6] In France, the debate began in 1965, with the publication of *Poor France*, a summary of recent findings on poverty. The Irish debate began slightly later, but in parallel fashion with a major conference on poverty in Kilkenny in 1971. Even in the apparently more prosperous West German Republic, there were comparable debates about the conditions of minorities like the homeless and the immigrant 'guest workers'.

Poverty and social inequality were found to persist, then, even in what might have been considered, according to certain perspectives at least, the most favourable conditions possible for their elimination. As the same study concluded, 'the period under discussion, i.e. the post-war decades, includes two decades in which the levels of economic growth in Europe as a whole well exceeded those of any earlier period for which records are available. . . .' These are developments which have often been associated with a reduction in relative inequalities. Moreover, 'the trends in income inequality and poverty which we are discussing took place in and during a period of unprecedentedly high rates of growth . . . in government expenditure. In other words, there was abundant national wealth and government activity to deal with the problems of excessive income inequality and poverty.[7] Yet, as in Britain and North America, the experience of the EEC member states was that both remained persistent phenomena. More recently published studies of poverty and of social mobility in Britain confirm these generally pessimistic conclusions.[8] In fact, as it has already been suggested, already by the early seventies, and more clearly by the mid seventies when the EEC anti-poverty programme was actually launched, the situation of the poor had been deteriorating in the worsening economic climate, accompanied by rising unemployment and exacerbated by cuts in public expenditure on welfare.

A further explanation that has been offered[9] for the EEC's interest in promoting the anti-poverty programme focuses upon the competition between the different organisations of the EEC itself – the Council of Ministers, representing the member states at the political level, the commission (the bureaucrats in Brussels) and the European parliament (originally an advisory, now an elected body), each trying to carve out distinctive roles for themselves. According to this interpretation, the EEC anti-poverty programme could be seen as the thin end of the wedge of increased EEC direct involvement in social policy; poverty represented, after all, an overtly altruistic set of issues around which the different organs could press their organisational self-interests.

Although commission officials (not surprisingly, of course) tended to refute any such imputations of empire building in the social policy field, this would in practice seem to be an increasingly significant area for policy analysis, because, in effect, whether or not there are further anti-poverty initiatives per se, the EEC has been, over time, and may be predicted to be, more extensively involved in social policy issues, if only in a minimum regulatory capacity. To argue this, however, is not to equate socio-economic and political pressures for EEC involvement in social policy regulation with the self-interest of officials, or even with any self-expanding tendencies of bureaucratic organisations.

The anti-poverty programme can perhaps be seen, too, in terms of a longer-term set of pressures around the nature of the EEC itself. These pressures include possible tensions arising from wider membership from Mediterranean countries, and current demands for budgetary reform, to reduce spending on the CAP and to increase the emphasis upon regional and social fund spending.

By the very nature of its location within a supranational organisation, the EEC anti-poverty programme cannot, however, simply be equated with national programmes. In particular the EEC did not, at that time, even include a directly elected assembly. Any relationship between anti-poverty programmes, the sponsorship of community action and the promotion of political constituencies or even pork barrels (such as have been traced, by Piven and Cloward,[10] for example, and Alinsky[11] in the US War on Poverty) cannot be assumed to be directly transferable. Nor can any direct relationship between anti-poverty programmes and the rationalisation of the provision of public welfare, a relationship which has been discussed in terms of British government sponsorship of self-help and voluntary action programmes in particular, the EEC not being, itself, a direct provider of welfare in any case.

The modesty of the budget (2.5 million units of account in 1975, or a fraction of the social fund which was itself some 6 per cent of EEC spending for the year, compared with 75 per cent for the CAP) was, however, more directly comparable. This modesty was similarly justified, too, in terms of the pilot/research status of the programme (despite the underdevelopment of evaluative research overall, which was not even formally organised until the 'ESPOIR' team was appointed in 1979, based at the University of Kent, four years after the programme was launched). In fact, as it turned out, however, the supposed 'pilot' status of the programme became more hotly contested over time, in part, at least, because the public expenditure cuts at national level made it decreasingly likely that successful project work would be continued, let alone generalised.

The theoretical ambiguity of the EEC anti-poverty programme had parallels, too, with experiences in previous programmes and this was critical in terms of subsequent struggles, including the projects' own struggles to define their legitimate spheres of concern and consequent action strategies according to alternative and competing perspectives.

So although the EEC anti-poverty programme, itself, has been criticised for being a hotchpotch collection of individual projects, rather than a more coherent programme,[12] it gave rise to struggles with broader relevance, both within and amongst the projects' struggles, which were also reflected at international level, particularly in the latter stages of the programme, when various of the individual projects worked through a process of developing a common and critical set of strategies.

At the outset of 1975, however, the EEC anti-poverty programme was described as being fluid. The programme was not systematically addressed even to the debates which had accompanied previous programmes, let alone to testing out alternative assumptions, whether about the definition and causation of poverty, or about the relevance or otherwise of area-based pilot community action programmes, however conceptualised, to tackle poverty. So given the problematic character of each of these concepts, involving as they do alternative and conflicting theoretical approaches, the possibilities for struggles around definitions and strategies were correspondingly considerable.

To summarise, in relation to the preceding discussions, exponents of individualist approaches resting upon functionalist notions of social stratification tended to conceptualise the programme in terms of whether or not the culture, morale, motivation and training of the poor in deprived areas could be improved so that social pathology and dependence upon social welfare could be reduced. Alternative approaches varied, but they included approaches which emphasised the potential relevance of the projects in terms of their capacity as community action programmes to support the deprived in organising to exert political pressure on their own behalf in immediate and limited terms, or as part of a longer-term perspective for challenging the very basis of the present structure of inequality of rewards and benefits in society (the hope expressed by George and Lawson (see note 12), for instance).

The final report from the commission itself to the council (December 1981) presents the different projects' approaches in terms of four alternative strategies which are characterised as social planning, community development, community action and assistance to specific groups and in specific fields. But in fact these four strategies overlapped and crossed the alternative theoretical approaches. So, for example, the area resource centres in Britain are offered as examples of community development, but these resource centres also included examples of support for community action as well as for social planning and service delivery, and the resource centres also included examples of support for these different modes of intervention in terms of alternative and competing theoretical perspectives. Within the projects, too, as it will emerge in more detail subsequently, there were not infrequently tensions and countervailing pressures, so that the final outcome, in terms of the theoretical model to be adopted, was by no means necessarily clear at the outset, nor even were the projects always internally consistent.

These tensions and internal inconsistencies represent an important caveat upon the accuracy of any attempts to categorise particular projects in terms of their theoretical perspective. Moreover individual projects had a range of potential reasons of their own for resisting specific categorisation of their theoretical orientation (not least of which was the necessity for member-state support for continued funding).

Within these limitations, however, certain broad tendencies are apparent. For example, there did appear to have been projects, or at least individuals within projects, who were working from within a framework which emphasised the necessity to reduce the social pathologies of the poor, in order to minimise their dependence upon welfare and to facilitate their integration into the wider society. For instance, the objective of 'Aide à Toute Détresse' (ATD), a voluntary organisation launched in the shanty towns on the outskirts of Paris, and the sponsor of four projects in the EEC anti-poverty programme (two in France, one in the Netherlands and one in the UK), has been characterised as the integration of the city's 'least favoured inhabitants into the life of the community'. ATD mobilises volunteers who 'devote themselves for several years at a time to live and work among the extreme poor'.

But while this goal of social integration was emphasised, ATD did also aim to assist the poor in 'articulating their needs to the rest of society, and to build a fruitful collaboration with sympathetic elements within it', which begins to move closer to a pluralist perspective, emphasising the necessity for increasing the bargaining power of the most disadvantaged social groups. Similarly the Dutch ATD project in Breda emphasised self-help amongst the poor and the need to promote their social integration, while, at the same time, supporting the development of locally controlled community organisations which raised consciousness of community issues, as well as themselves providing self-help services, such as children's clubs.

At the other end of the pluralist spectrum, in contrast, were projects which emphasised the development of the organisational capacity and consciousness of the poor, including those which linked this to wider strategies to tackle the present structure of socio-economic and political inequality. One of the most challenging examples was provided by the Centre for Social Medicine, based in Guigliano, Naples. The Guigliano project started from a radical, structural definition of poverty. Community action, then, was, for this project, necessary, in terms of the development of concrete struggles, which included real intermediate gains for local people, but which raised their aspirations for more radical changes too, which at the same time developed organisational capacities to press for these wider changes.

The Guigliano project focused upon social medicine in the broadest holistic sense, with a key concern for preventative medicine, and the promotion of positive good health as contrasted with a narrower definition of health in terms of the treatment of ill-health. So health and safety at work, and the elimination of industrial pollution, poor housing and environment and malnutrition, were crucial concerns, as well as the more self-evidently health service-related programmes of preventative health, and health education for mothers and children.

The project was concerned, however, not only with the demystification of 'medical' problems with socio-economic implications, but with the development of what the project workers termed a process of 'critical dialogue' between project workers and the client community. What did this 'critical dialogue' process actually entail? Typically, local people would present themselves to the project with 'needs' expressed, for example, in technical/medical terms. They would ask for drugs or injections, for instance, to alleviate specific symptoms. While the project workers would always take these requests/expressions of 'felt need' seriously, they did not, however, accept the clients' initial formulation of 'need' as final or unproblematic. On the contrary, through developing a 'critical dialogue' the goal was to initiate a process of unwrapping these 'needs', and uncovering, where this was appropriate, the underlying socio-economic and cultural causes of the presenting symptoms, together with the potential for collective solutions – for example the self-organisation of women to tackle the social and cultural pressures which were leading to depression or hysteria amongst women – rather than simply treating these symptoms with drugs.

Overall, the Guigliano project's approach could be character-ised as radical both in theory and in practice, based upon a structural (although not structuralist) analysis of the causes of poverty and ill-health. And this was linked to a strategic approach to community action, which required respect for the client community's own definitions, consciousness and self-organisation (rather than discussing these as merely the products of 'false consciousness'), yet which involved the development of a process of dialogue between the client community and an alternative theoretical perspective.

Similarly, in some respects, the Irish Combat Poverty projects, for example, were launched on the basis of an attempt at a co-ordinated approach (which predated the EEC anti-poverty pro-gramme itself) starting from the stated assumption that:[13]

> It is fundamental to the philosophy of the programme that poverty in Irish society should be recognised as largely the result of inequality and that its eventual elimination . . . will require a redistribution of resources and power in society.

In practice, however, the Irish Combat Poverty programme illustrated, within itself, the wider tensions and countervailing pressures for definition and redefinition – for a radical approach on the one hand, and a recovery of the 'middle-ground' on the other. As one of the participants has explained, in relation to the experience of one of the projects within the Combat Poverty programme in Dublin '(there was, underlying the project's strategy) the assumption that popular participation and radical socio-economic transformations were requirements of any anti-poverty strategy.' So this project mobilised popular organisation and political activity, for example, facilitating the production of an 'alternative local people's plan' to challenge redevelopment proposals for the area:[14]

> These activities tended to eclipse the social service functions

which some social policy makers in fact considered more suitable for a Combat Poverty project, services consistent with the work of professional social workers, with the identification of so-called marginal groups in the community, with information and advice work.

Far from being a coherent, let alone a consistently radical, package of projects, at least at national level, in fact the Irish programme contained alternative and conflicting approaches and strategies. Nor did the institutional arrangements, it has been suggested, promote the resolution of these tensions. For example, there were two inner city projects in the Irish Republic, administered under the aegis of the National Committee on Pilot Schemes to Combat Poverty. This committee, in turn, split up the two inner city schemes into a South Dublin project run directly by the committee and a North Dublin project run by a local board of management. So far from encouraging unified approaches to inner city poverty, EEC anti-poverty funds were channelled into Ireland, city by city; funds were even separately administered within one city. The two Northern Ireland projects were separate again. The logic of this, for an island with a total population of a mere 4.8 million, and two cities only 110 miles apart, is difficult to discern:[15]

In this regard the EEC Anti-Poverty Programme was not surprisingly unable to transcend existing political barriers and promote concerted strategies to tackle poverty in Ireland as a whole. The opportunity for collective inner city inter-project work was not so much lost, as handicapped from the outset, by the establishment of new institutions: community projects – devoid of any vehicle for inter-project research, comparison, debate or meeting, thus appearing to perpetuate the notion that decline of inner city working class communities is city-specific and geographically unique.

This lack of effective co-ordination, even within one national programme, in Ireland reflected, in turn, the situation within the EEC anti-poverty programme as a whole. And as it has already been suggested the programme has been described, perhaps not unfairly, as a 'hotch-potch'.

The initial projects were chosen for a variety of reasons through the member states, rather than from any inherent attempt at rationality. And once established the commission lacked the means of promoting effective co-ordination subsequently with the exception of a conference, annual meetings of project leaders, and certain discussions on the lessons of the programme subsequently (1981/82). In fact this lack of effective co-ordination was not an oversight on the part of the responsible officials; the case for a European dimension to the programme emerged clearly from the early papers. Rather, this points once again to the structural difficulties of achieving co-ordination on social policy initiatives between different member states, in any case, let alone between projects which both within and between themselves contained conflicting approaches and strategies.

In the event, it was the projects, themselves, which began to develop their own network of co-ordination. As the refunding issue loomed large on their individual agendas, in 1979, separate projects came together and formed their own organisation (ESCAP). The initial purpose was to press for refunding, and they lobbied with considerable energy and impact, especially in the European parliament. (Local community activists were even involved, on a cross-national basis, in a demonstration in support of refunding in Brussels.) But in the process, and in part, at least, because of the expectation that co-ordinated bids would stand a greater chance of success, ESCAP also came to play a role in developing strategies for co-ordinated inter-project work. Common approaches were agreed, for instance, on programmes to tackle employment, housing and health. There were also plans for common approaches to welfare rights and service integration.

The fact that even these programmes could be agreed, in view of the disparate nature of the projects, may, in itself, be remarkable. How far such joint strategies could have been implemented inevitably remains problematic, since this was never attempted systematically. Nor did all the projects take part, by any means. ATD, for example, were minimally represented at these discussions. Inasmuch as there was any discernible theoretical orientation of the projects involved, this tended to represent elements within the pluralist perspective and at the radical end of the pluralist spectrum, although there were considerable differences, even amongst those who were involved.

Subsequently, however, there were further interchanges, including exchange visits between projects of relatively similar orientation (Guigliano, Naples and Waterford, Ireland, for example). And more broadly, there was certainly subsequent interest in the experiences and approaches of particular projects, both amongst former EEC anti-poverty programme projects and beyond, amongst community activists more widely.

The British roots

The discussion, so far, has centred upon the EEC dimension of the UK programme and the area resource centre's place within this. In fact, however, the notion of developing these particular resource centres, in the first place, had indigenous roots, too, located within British community work debates. As Chapter 1 has already outlined, the call for the establishment of area resource centres (backed by a national centre) to offer support to community groups emerged out of the deliberations of a committee under the chairpersonship of Lord Boyle, known as the community work group, sponsored by the Calouste Gulbenkian Foundation representing, as it has already been suggested, the 'middle-ground', or at least an attempt to hold the middle, pluralist ground, against the polarising tendencies of first the radical challenges from the left and subsequently from the new right. So the Boyle committee attempted to straddle the range of pluralist approaches to community work and community action.

After a review of the way in which community work and community action had grown in recent years, the concluding chapter of the Boyle report identified areas of need in the community work field and proposals for meeting them. In the view of the community work group, the overriding need was to provide support for the development of emerging community groups, including support for community work practitioners and teachers. The specific proposal for a national and for local resource centres has already been outlined in Chapter 1.

It was eventually decided to push for the funding of a total of six area community resource centres, either directly or by recommending their application to other funding sources, including the EEC anti-poverty programme, as in the case of the South

Wales anti-poverty action centre, Govan area resource centre and the London community work service. Those funded directly by the Voluntary Service Unit in the Home Office (VSU) were the British Council of Churches community resource unit and two centres resulting from an application from the former Young Volunteer Foundation, now Community Projects' Foundation (CPF), for centres in Manchester and in Tyne and Wear.

All six centres eventually took part in a joint monitoring exercise, in addition to the evaluation which the EEC's team, ESPOIR, carried out on the three EEC-funded resource centres, from 1979. It was this joint monitoring committee which was responsible for generating much of the empirical material which is included in this case study in the rest of this chapter and in Chapters 4, 5 and 6. By definition, the first stage of the area resource centre evaluation process started from a situation which defied the adoption of an ideal experimental design. The centres to be studied were chosen before the research had been planned; they were neither selected for their representative character nor even because of their common level of funding, size of area or services offered. The centres did not even become operational simultaneously, nor did the research begin until some of the work had been going on for two years. Even more significantly, area resource centres started from no clearly articulated hypotheses, either about the concept of community and the relevance of community work in general, or more specifically about small area approaches to tackling poverty. On the contrary in fact, these represented precisely some of the key arenas to be contested both amongst the centres and within them.

Finally, whilst these area resource centres which emerged in the wake of the Calouste Gulbenkian sponsored Boyle committee shared elements, at least of a common parentage, they were by no means the only experiments of their type in Britain in the mid to late seventies. A further study of resource centres, sponsored again by the Calouste Gulbenkian Foundation and the Voluntary Services Unit for comparative purposes (1980/81), listed a considerable range of projects bearing the name of 'resource centre'. These varied from centres which were effectively neighbourhood centres (e.g., the Creggan resource centre in Derry) through to specialist support services, and resource centres which served specific but geographically disparate interests and groups (such as the Community Council's resource centre in Glasgow). The term 'resource centre' then, far from being confined to the Boyle committee's initiatives, was, in fact, being applied to more or less the range of community work and community action support services in the UK, by the end of the seventies.

By the late seventies, one end of this spectrum was characterised by the practice and the publications of a grouping of resource centres, several of which were rooted in the inter-project work of the CDPs (although others had been related to the EEC initiative itself). The network grouping of these centres emerged, committed to a radical and non-sectarian practice, and particularly concerned to relate community-based struggles (defined in relation to a class analysis) with trade union-based work-place struggles, as well as in the women's movement. The network describes its own goals in the following terms:[16]

> Our twin aims are to help working class groups tackling concrete problems
> (a) to gain practical improvements in their immediate circumstances
> (b) to learn more about their situation while trying, collectively, to change it.
> The way we work with groups is as important as the services we offer
>
>> we are accountable to the groups with whom we work, and work in close dialogue with them;
>> we do not come in as 'outside experts' but work alongside the groups as committed advisers;
>> we try to build up the strength and self-sufficiency of the groups we work with by passing on our knowledge, skills and experience in as understandable and useful ways as possible, and. . . .
>> . . . we consciously try to build links and a sharing of experience between different sections of the trade union, community and women's movements. We also try to develop a fuller understanding of the inter-connections between issues at the workplace, in the home and in the community.

The starting point for our work with groups is nearly always an issue felt to be a source of grievance and priority is given to responding to a request for help from a group which has identified the issue it wants to tackle. On other occasions the resource centre will have identified an issue as important, and will initiate the contact with groups affected to check if they recognise it as a problem to be tackled. In either case the dialogue between researchers and activists will inevitably move the thinking of both partners on beyond the original starting-point and begin to explore the context and underlying causes of the immediate presenting problem.

Because we assist groups which are trying to remedy grievances and improve their situation, our work frequently has political implications. We do not shy away from acknowledging this, or deny that our research and advice has an important influence on the action groups choose to take. However, our approach is entirely non-sectarian, and is governed by our accountability to the groups we work with, and to our elected management or advisory committees. It should be clear (from the preceding paragraphs) that we are committed to democratic and educational methods of work, and not to political manipulation in any shape or form.

As the network developed, it represented, then, an alternative analysis, and potentially an alternative reference point for the resource centres which had emerged from the aftermath of the Boyle report. But the network was not, of course, the only alternative external reference point. Resource centres, as it has already been suggested, covered a broader range of theoretical approaches and strategies.

So how did the area resource centres within the EEC anti-poverty programme respond to these varying influences and pressures?

Defining objectives and operationalising strategies

Despite the fact that there were differences between the resource centres in terms of their size, funding sources, areas of operations and management structures, they shared some parallel dilemmas too, as each came to try to operationalise their varying initial briefs. Typically, each set of objectives was far too broad for the resources which had actually been provided, so that the project workers could have filled their working days in concentrating upon any one objective to the effective exclusion of the remaining goals. And more fundamentally, as has already been argued, the Boyle group's conceptual definitions were amenable to alternative interpretations which could be used to justify varying and ultimately conflicting strategies in practice. The rest of this chapter looks at the resource centres' resulting efforts to establish their own strategies and priorities, within the constraints of the different interests to which they were accountable. Whilst the main focus of the rest of this case study is upon the three centres which were funded through the EEC anti-poverty programme, illustrations are included too, from the remaining three centres which emerged in the wake of the Boyle report.

Govan Area Resource Centre (GARC), Glasgow

The Govan Area Resource Centre, GARC (located in Glasgow), started with a broad range of objectives, relating to the general provision of information, training and exchanges of experiences and ideas, within the framework of providing support to community groups and relevant professionals and agencies.

Local groups had only been consulted after these general outlines had been proposed (in the negotiations following the Boyle report) so that they tended to accept them (or not as the case may be) as part of a package, without necessarily sharing any clearly agreed view as to definitions or priorities. Operationalisation, then, was potentially problematic, and there was initial debate about the centre's purpose. Early on, strategic decisions were affected, too, by local political considerations; for example, local redevelopment plans were not eventually accorded a high priority, because of the fear of jeopardising other project relationships, especially with the local authority, if redevelopment was a major area of concern – an illustration once again of the difficulties of holding the middle-ground, whilst responding to local working-class aspirations and definitions of needs.

The development of the centre's strategy also became affected by more general political debates within and around the local

Labour Party, which began to spill over into the debates then taking place in the management committee.

Once the resource centre was there, though, attempting to operate in an area where different organisations and factions operated, these tensions were inevitably exacerbated, as the centre's own funds and resources became an object for in-fighting. By 1979, these tensions within the management committee had become so serious that an outside consultant had to be called in. At one stage, these tensions spread within the centre's workers, too, before they were resolved.

Meanwhile, back in 1977, the centre began work with three staff focusing initially upon developing information resources, including a resource library (which could not in practice be staffed adequately for lack of manpower), and a bi-monthly newsletter. Local groups, such as tenants' associations and a group organising a toy library, were also able to use the equipment and to obtain other forms of support such as funding advice and small grants.

Support for tenants' groups did not become the main focus of the project work, however, top priority being given to the employment issue. The development of GARC's employment strategy is discussed in more detail in Chapter 5.

While unemployment was indisputedly a crucial problem in Govan, and a rapidly worsening one, the resource centre's approach was initially loosely-defined – symptomatic, in fact, of the resource centre's launching problems more generally. GARC's first initiative – an employment study group in Govan – set out to consider the issue in broad terms, including a focus upon deindustrialisation and the destruction of jobs together with resistance to these processes, and there was also some potential focus upon job creation within co-operatives and/or community enterprise ventures. As Chapter 5 describes in more detail, it emerged however that such a broad set of objectives could not be contained at that time within one project, and as it eventually turned out the job creation goals, for a time at least, won out at the expense of the interest in job preservation, and the work with organised labour as such. Back in 1977, however, the problems associated with such choices had not been appreciated, and the project workers and the management committee were still attempting to combine a broader set of objectives.

Community Work Service (CWS), London

In contrast, the London Voluntary Council's Community Work Service (CWS) started with six workers (plus two training workers, funded by the Inner London Education Authority), more than double the staff resources of GARC. The problems of establishing priorities as part of the broader choice of strategies was just as acute, however, if anything more so, because CWS was to service the metropolitan area, with some six million inhabitants, and a plethora of relevant organisations at local, borough and regional/GLC level.

Overall, CWS tended to focus upon strengthening organisations and potential links at this latter level, on the grounds that this had been the least developed area of work, whilst being the most appropriate level for support from a regional resource centre. This aspect of the CWS's strategy is set out in more detail in Chapter 4, with examples of their information and training work.

CWS's metropolitan location also affected the form of the project's management, since local management at such a level, with a locality of over six million inhabitants, would have been particularly problematic. User control, in fact, only really emerged as a viable possibility in relation to more specific off-shoot project work such as the CWS support work for the Campaign for Family Housing (discussed in Chapter 6).

Being situated within the London Voluntary Service Council (LVSC), with its own interpretations of community work and its own specific focus upon voluntary organisations, and volunteering more generally, was also clearly a potential source of influence as CWS's own definitions and strategies were being developed. Clearly, too, the association with LVSC was a possible source of definitions from the viewpoint of users or potential user organisations (whether positively or negatively, depending upon their own stance), especially in the early stages before CWS had developed its own separate and recognisable identity. The information work (including the newsletter) and the training programme were crucial here, not only in providing services to local community groups and workers, but in putting across CWS's own distinctive image at the same time.

In addition to the basic information and training prongs of the strategy, CWS also developed support work for specific groups, such as a prisoners' wives and families society (for whom CWS arranged fund-raising help and auditing of their accounts), Harambee II, a training project for unemployed West Indian youth (which was helped with consultancy) and the Ferndale project, a community project and day nursery in Brixton.

Over time, however, it became clear that even eight workers could not possibly respond to every request of this type from local projects, let alone do so while maintaining any metropolitan information and resource support service. At this point, priority was given to support for metropolitan-level support work, especially for linking campaigns which were trying to operate at metropolitan level. For example, the all-London campaign against school closures was a group of parents, teachers and school governers, and relevant community groups, who were organising to retain thirty schools in Inner London which were under threat of closure. Whilst the campaign was active, CWS provided secretarial and information support. Similarly, the campaign to improve public transport was a federation of groups and public transport users and workers concerned to prevent further reductions in service and losses of jobs. CWS collected and distributed information on a co-ordinated basis. A further example of CWS's support for community groups operating at metropolitan level is provided in the case study of the campaign for family housing/homes in Central London (Chapter 6), which was organising resistance to the break-up of working-class communities in Central London.

But even restricting community work support to metropolitan groups did not, of course, ultimately resolve CWS's problems. The campaign for family housing/homes in Central London, for example, came to dominate a large proportion of one worker's time. In the absence of sufficient funding to hive off such projects with their own independent worker, CWS inevitably reached the point when support for any new metropolitan campaign would have placed impossible strains even upon their apparently relatively generous quota of eight workers in total.

The extent of the resources available, including the number of project workers, clearly affected the different strategies which each area resource centre developed, but in no way to the exclusion of other aspects of their strategic choices, including, of course, the balance of theoretical perspectives, amongst the project workers and their management committees and the impact which these had on their selection of priorities.

South Wales Anti-Poverty Action Centre (SWAPAC)

SWAPAC seems to have provided the most explicit set of definitions, objectives and strategies, largely because the centre underwent an internal review process, as a result of which there was a major change of direction. Strategies were shifted and priorities narrowed down to concentrate upon fewer but key issues around jobs, housing, legal services and social services, including health – a process of review which clearly involved critical discussions both amongst the team of seven and the management committee.

SWAPAC started with an explicit focus upon poverty, within the context of industrial decline and the consequent processes of out-migration from the South Wales mining valleys. Having located the structural causes within the local economy, as the impact of the wider industrial rationalisation process destroyed jobs and incomes, SWAPAC focused upon a twofold strategy, emphasising, in contrast, the role of self-help on the one hand, and policy feedback on the other. This policy feedback was to bring the plight of South Wales to the politicians' attention, on the assumption that such information would lead to relevant policy-formation, including increasing public expenditure and investment (despite all the indications to the contrary from the broader policy trends of the public expenditure cuts of the mid seventies).

The self-help prong of SWAPAC's strategy was to develop new democratic and co-operative social relations, through employment or housing co-operatives, for example. Somehow such developments were supposed to begin a process which would lead to the eradication of structural poverty. 'Increased resources', it was argued, 'could not themselves resolve the structural phenomena of poverty', so that it would be necessary 'to help to create new forms of social relations, by people working together on issues of mutual concern, particularly projects which enable poor people to take greater control of their life situations.'[17]

What did such an approach mean in practice, in the establishment of priorities and strategies? SWAPAC's team was basically a team of specialists – in law, housing, welfare rights, community work and political economy – so that each team member tended to work within a particular specialism and with particular types of organisations. Because of this diversity and because they were working in a very dispersed geographical area, team members would meet relatively rarely, except at the weekly team meetings. Initially then, SWAPAC's interventions covered a broad and disparate range of issues and activities.

Industry and employment were given some attention in terms of developing co-operative employment creation projects, particularly those aimed at securing job creation project funds from the Manpower Services Commission (MSC). By the end of 1976, fifteen groups had been helped to prepare such applications and more were in the pipeline. The implications of such an approach to employment together with some of the reasons for SWAPAC's subsequent change of employment strategy are discussed in more detail in Chapter 5.

By 1977, however, doubts were being raised. Resources from the MSC for job creation projects (JCP) were proving very difficult to obtain and when they were available, the way in which their use was prescribed led to serious reservations. Employment could only be provided for a year under JCP and the fact that this was often insufficient time to launch a co-operative led to the whole purpose of the programme being questioned.

More fundamentally, the emphasis upon co-operative employment creation was taking increasing resources of time and energy; yet it was at the same time taking SWAPAC further away from key sections of the local 'community' which they were hoping to resource, particularly the labour movement which was typically more concerned, at that period, with job preservation struggles (particularly as the major nationalised industries in the area continued to shed labour as part of the industrial rationalisation process). Consequently support for job preservation struggles, as part of a wider strategy for supporting the labour movement, became increasingly emphasised in the second phase of SWAPAC's strategic approach.

There were parallels in the shifts around SWAPAC's housing strategy. Initially, the emphasis had been on assisting self-help groups, either to develop housing associations or to set up management co-operatives on council estates. This strategy came into question increasingly, particularly as it became clear that, as a result of the cuts in public expenditure, housing associations and co-ops were gaining no new resources for the area, but were effectively competing with the public sector where the majority of working-class tenants were housed.

Members of the SWAPAC team were, by this time, arguing that the centre must become increasingly selective in the groups and issues which were to be supported because much community action, including some of that supported by SWAPAC in the first phase, involved 'the kind of self-help that results in people merely administering their own poverty in the illusion that they are taking active measures in arriving at its elimination.'[18]

SWAPAC, it was argued, should not concentrate upon increasing local competition for decreasing resources, whether through housing co-ops competing with local authority tenants or through employment co-ops being seen as potentially cutting across trade union job preservation struggles. Instead, the focus should be upon supporting local initiatives, which included both immediate and achievable goals, and the potential for developing a longer-term process of broadening perspectives. Part of this broadening process was thought to relate to developing linkages both between individuals and between different community groups sharing common problems – to overcome the individual-isation process and to develop mutual solidarity. (Chapter 4 discusses SWAPAC's attempts to develop welfare rights' organis-ations and provides an example of this later approach. Chapter 6 provides further examples of linking work through SWAPAC's support for the development of the South Wales Association of Tenants.)

Finally, the new strategy was to develop links between community groups and organised labour, the labour movement having, it was argued, its own political tradition, albeit an underdeveloped tradition, in terms of the way in which it was applied to issues which had been defined as falling within the sphere of the community, rather than the workplace. Some of the implications of these strategic changes are discussed again in Chapter 5, in relation to the employment work. Research to support joint trade union action around cuts in public expenditure, particularly cuts in the health service, similarly provided further examples of this shift in SWAPAC's strategic direction, in practice.

To summarise, SWAPAC's overall shift in orientation provides, perhaps, the clearest illustration of the conflicting pressures and the struggles between competing theoretical perspectives, from an emphasis upon self-help and participation, through to a strategy which related more closely to a radical perspective. This latter perspective was also explicitly concerned, as the case studies in Chapters 4, 5 and 6 demonstrate, to start from the individual's and the groups' perceptions of their problems and needs and then to support them in their own 'learning through experience' – the very antithesis in fact of the supposed rejection of the neighbourhood base, with which radical community workers have on occasion been charged.

The three remaining centres

While the specific patterns in the remaining three centres differed, none of them avoided the conflicting pressures and tensions experienced in the first three centres. In Manchester, for example, the area resource centre (MARC) responded initially, by attempting to preserve a 'low profile'.

The emphasis at first was upon the provision of practical services, such as printing, duplicating, and typing for local community groups in Greater Manchester. Initially, MARC made available a duplicator, electric stencil cutter, photocopier, typewriters, a guillotine and a large supply of different grades of paper at cost price. Later, a second duplicator, tape recorder, loudhailer, calculator and a van for hire were added to the resources available to groups. The equipment was soon heavily used as word spread throughout Greater Manchester. In the first year, sixty-six groups used MARC regularly and thirty-nine used it on a one-off basis. The groups were largely based in the Manchester District and were mainly tenants' or housing groups, although initially there was some demand, too, from play organisations and advice centres.

A newsletter was launched in 1975, covering both local community groups' news and events and articles on relevant national issues, such as major changes in social security and housing law.

Work with local groups and with federations proved more problematic, however, raising inevitably more substantial dilemmas about priorities and definitions. In the first year, MARC did set about assisting and servicing a number of city-wide campaigns which were developing at the time. Subsequently, however, MARC was more reluctant to play a leading role in similar ventures, although the centre did continue to provide information to joint campaigns on a city-wide basis. The solution, then, at this stage, was abstention from potentially contentious issues, a strategy of keeping firmly within the 'middle-ground'.

Like MARC (in Manchester) and CWS (in Greater London), the Tyne and Wear resource centre was set up to cover a metropolitan area (with over a million inhabitants), rather than a locality (such as Govan), but with only two workers initially (and subsequently four workers).

In practice, the Tyne and Wear strategy involved the provision of hardware too (such as access to duplicators and a silk screen press) and information resources, including a newspaper *Resource Post*. As in MARC, local groups used the centre for a variety of purposes, including meeting there, and running off their leaflets, posters and newsletters.

Tyne and Wear differed from MARC, however, in that the centre placed more emphasis upon going beyond the provision of information, including providing both research and community work support for a range of groups, campaigns and federations, especially on housing issues where the centre soon developed a recognised expertise. For example, when Newcastle Trades Council established an action committee to oppose the cuts in public expenditure in 1975, the Tyne and Wear resource centre became actively involved in support work, collecting and disseminating relevant materials.

A major commitment was made to support and service the North East Tenants' Organisation (NETO). NETO was set up in September 1977 at a conference of tenants' groups as a result of a decision at a national tenants' conference to set up regional organisations. Tyne and Wear resource centre was approached to help to organise the conference; and subsequently the resource centre agreed to service and support NETO. Over thirty groups had by this time affiliated, from the north-east region. NETO has been involved in a range of activities, including both community action and self-education of its members on housing and related issues. For example, weekend courses have been organised for members of NETO at the Northern College, Barnsley, in order to provide opportunities for issues and experience to be explored in depth. These courses proved very popular and have been well attended by tenants' representatives.

One of the most stimulating aspects of these 'educational' experiences proved to be the exchange with representatives from tenants' organisations elsewhere, including Coventry and South Wales. The South Wales Association of Tenants similarly put great value on these exchanges, as they described in the interviews for the case study in Chapter 6.

The exchanges were also part of the background of the development of the national housing liaison committee (discussed again in Chapter 6 in relation to the CWS supported campaign for family housing/homes in Central London).

The Tyne and Wear centre's definitions of its role, then, could hardly have been located at that end of the spectrum characterised by self-help, volunteering and feedback to local authorities. The implications of these definitions and the centre's ensuing strategies were not lost on the projects' sponsors or their client groups either. Some of these implications can be traced, for example, in terms of complaints about the centre by certain councillors and by the less than enthusiastic support which the centre received when negotiating for refunding. On the other hand, these implications were clearly not lost on the local labour movement or local tenants' organisations either. After VSU funding ended in March 1980, the Tyne and Wear centre continued to operate, albeit on a shoe-string, with alternative funding (from War on Want), relying on support from volunteers and sharing premises with the Newcastle Trades Council sponsored, unemployed workers centre.

In contrast, finally, the sixth centre was a resource unit, located within the British Council of Churches (BCC), a unit which could be considered, perhaps, as shifting in response to conflicting pressures, in the opposite direction. Initially, the project worker emphasised the relevance of the resource unit in terms of supporting community action, as contrasted with an emphasis on the churches themselves and more directly theological concerns. In relation to the work of the unit itself, the interim report argued, for example, that:[19]

> We have sought to relate to those who have, or are seeking to have, a methodical approach to enabling those in such situations (i.e. of deprivation) to influence the environment in which they live, enabling people to define their problems, make changes and gain the resources to which they are justly entitled.
>
> Sometimes, we have been concerned, therefore, to see how the churches' resources of money, plant and people can be best utilised in support of community initiatives and self-help. We have been concerned with the interrelation between church and community and with a wide variety of strategies and approaches. The advisory committee has also recognised that 'good' community work leads to an involvement in power and politics.

In practice, this meant that that the unit contacted and supported over a hundred local community action initiatives, based from churches or Christian organisations. In addition to, and supporting this priority to community action, the unit provided back-up material, including the production of packs on particular topics, and a newsletter three times a year carrying a range of information and case studies. A handbook was also produced, *Understanding Inequality*, relating the causes of social inequality to the potential contribution which community action could make to tackling them.

Although this support for community action was the key focus for the unit initially, the secretary did also attempt to maintain links with the central denominational bodies of the churches, and with the relevant department of the BCC itself. Combining these different sets of priorities proved an uneasy balancing act, however. In fact, the internal review reporting on the first phase of the funding argued that the unit's communication and contact with relevant central bodies of the member churches had been insufficient.

In practice, subsequently, after the first secretary left, in the second phase, the unit did shift its priorities in this direction, working more closely with the churches, rather than with local community action initiatives. The first definitions of community work and community action and the consequent strategy came to be reshaped then, to fit more closely with the goals and interests of the sponsoring church organisations. The unit, incidentally, was the only one of the six centres to retain VSU funding after 1981 (when the matching EEC funding ran out).

Even the strategy of the resource unit within the BCC then, was affected by parallel pressures and the conflicts of theoretical approach which have already been traced, both in relation to the EEC anti-poverty programme in general, and the three UK area resource centres which provide more specific case study material in the following chapters.

Part two

The resource centres in action

4 Information, advocacy and community action

The information and advocacy project work which is discussed in this chapter represented central, core functions for the resource centres, as envisaged in the Boyle/Gulbenkian tradition. As Chapter 3 has set out, the Community Work Group re-emphasised the 1968 Gulbenkian study group's overall pluralist approach to the 'broader consideration of the role of community work in a democratic society'. Community work was, the group reaffirmed, a 'means of giving life to local democracy'.[1] Central to such an ultimate objective was the significance which the group placed upon participation mechanisms, in general, and upon the communication systems which would be required both to inform those to be affected by public policy proposals and to 'extend the means available to a wide range of groups in the community to express their views'.

The main needs of potentially participating community groups were summarised by the report as follows: 'Information, advisory and supporting services, and training, together with funding and opportunities for local and wider exchanges of views and experiences'. This chapter concentrates upon case studies dealing with the resource centres' experiences in relation to the first three of these functions, focusing upon a newsletter, a training course on community health, and a welfare rights advocacy programme – projects which represented, typically, core activities for all these centres. Before discussing these examples in more detail, however, it will be relevant to their location to summarise certain strands in contemporary debates about the relationship between information, and information services, more generally, on the one hand, and the question of democracy, on the other. For, whilst the Gulbenkian Community Work Group's approach concurred with official thinking on public participation in general (for example, the Skeffington report 1969[2]) was characterised in the group's report as an example of a positive response to community pressure for a proper say in decisions), this approach was, as it has already been suggested, far from representing an unproblematic consensus. As Chapter 2 has argued, 'participation' mechanisms and information services were both advocated and evaluated in terms of varying ultimate goals arising from alternative theoretical perspectives. Information, training and advocacy work, then, involved potentially varying interpretations as these common core strands were operationalised.

The 'right to know' has been advocated, for example, as this chapter will suggest, not simply as a prerequisite for citizen participation, but as part of a broader concern with open government and the freedom of information on the one hand, and in the campaigns for press freedom (and for an alternative newspaper to combat the increasing monopolisation of the media) on the other. Both these approaches rest upon critiques, albeit varying critiques, of pluralist assumptions about the nature of the social democratic state, acknowledging, as they do, that freedom of information is not merely or even predominantly a technical problem requiring cybernetic adjustment.

In fact, then, the Community Work Group's case for expanding information services in the early seventies represented one amongst several strands arising in some cases from differing theoretical stances with the demand for expanded information services as their common meeting point.

As it has already been suggested, too, a concern for the effective functioning of social democracy had roots which were established in sociological literature, well before the more overt and politically articulated concern of the mid-to-late sixties (the era of the US War on Poverty's 'maximum feasible participation' and of the Skeffington report and CDP in the UK).

C. Wright Mills, for example, developed his critique of pluralist assumptions about the state in the USA in the mid 1950s. *The Power Elite*[3] (1956) came to the conclusion that the classic model of participatory democracy was 'a set of images out of a fairy tale', bearing no correspondence with the contemporary USA. This was not at all, he argued, because of some grand conspiracy, or even that the class backgrounds of the elite could simply be equated with their rule in terms of their own class interests.

Democracy was at risk, however, he argued, as power, including the means of communication, was effectively concentrated in fewer hands – where 'far fewer people express opinions than receive them, and where the individual lacks effective means to contact the channels of communication or even to respond'.

'The political structure of a democratic state requires the public', yet public opinion was, he believed, becoming increasingly passive and dependent on the mass media.[4] While for Mills, then, restrictions on information and particularly the lack of genuine competition of views in the media were a major block to the operation of democratic structures, this was free from representing the sole cause of the problem, involving, as it did, the biases of power, and the associated class interests inherent in contemporary social democracies.

At the end of the sixties, Miliband's *The State in Capitalist Society* (dedicated, incidentally, to the memory of C. Wright Mills) developed the analysis of these elements of imperfect competition in the capitalist state in relation to the class interests of the dominant class. In particular, Miliband discusses the apparent contradiction between the overtly free competition of news and information in the field of communication – the press, the written word generally, radio, television, the cinema and the theatre. Whilst Miliband makes clear that the media *cannot* simply be considered the mouthpiece of the government of the day ('controversial news do find their way'), he emphasised that 'the notion of pluralist diversity and competition equilibrium is . . . rather superficial and misleading.'[5] For example, he discusses the hostility of the major British national daily newspapers to any politics left of 'the milder forms of social democracy,[6] their history of objections to any enlargement of the public sector and their record in terms of reporting trade union affairs and strikes in particular.

'The nature of the contribution which the mass media make to that political climate is determined by the influences which weigh most heavily upon them. There are a number of such influences – and they all work in the same conservative and conformist direction.'[7] Similar arguments appeared in the TUC Media Working Group's paper 'A Cause for Concern',[8] which examined bias in media coverage of industrial disputes in January and February 1979. Such notions about the role of the media in general in legitimating the predominance of the values of the market economy have, in fact, been expressed in a range of political analyses, including the controversial findings of the Glasgow University Media Group.[9]

In addition the earlier May Day Manifesto (1968),[10] for example, pointed to what the authors believed to be a deterioration in this situation as a result of the increasing monopolisation of the media and their accompanyingly decreasing diversity: 'During the 1960's, six national papers have been shut down, although five of them had circulations of well over a million. . . . It is a paradox of the modern means of communication, which are so essential if a complicated society is to know and speak to itself, that they are so expensive that their control passes inevitably, unless there is public intervention, into minority hands which then use them to impose their own views of the world.'[11]

By 1978, 85 per cent of newspaper-reading adults read four papers only (and three of these were generally anti-labour and trade union). Nearly 30 per cent of the adult population, moreover, did not even read a newspaper at all.[12]

This, then, was the context in which at both national and local community level there have been campaigns to develop an alternative media, whether through a new national newspaper and/or through the hundreds of community newspapers which have been established over the last decade or so. As the Directory of Social Change (1977), commented, 'the total number of community papers must now be measured in hundreds, though not yet in thousands.'[13] Community newspapers were by the mid seventies, as *Community Action* magazine has also argued, significant as part of the 'propaganda battle'.[14]

A further strand in the growing concern about the relationship between freedom of information and democracy has been represented by the mounting pressure for more open government, including pressure for a British Freedom of Information Act. The present Official Secrets Act and more specifically, as Michael Meacher for example has pointed out, even 'the rules which regulate how the authorities shall normally conduct themselves', operate against the public's right to know – 'Whitehall's short-way with democracy'.

A major element which Meacher identified in this failure arose as a result of a process which he describes as the 'selective restriction on the dissemination of information, which keeps the power of decision-making limited in fewer hands, and rebuts undesired Ministerial or Public intrusion especially into the most sensitive areas of policy'.[15]

In his essay on the secret state[16] E.P. Thompson goes further still in relating the official secrets policy and media distortions to what he considers to be the increasing statism of the past decades. Recent changes in the jury system, for example, are taken by Thompson as symptomatic of an increasing emphasis on law and order at the expense of civil liberties.

At this point, the discussion may seem to be diverging substantially from the starting point, the concern with access to information and information services per se. In practice, however, these broader perspectives on the 'right to know' in relation to the operations of the democratic structures of Western social democracies do relate to substantial differences of approach in the provision of information for advocacy and training services. One model of these differences, in practice, has been offered by Butcher, Cole and Glen[17] on the basis of their consumer study of information advice services offered in West Cumbria via the CDP project. Butcher and his colleagues concluded that information-giving was conceptionalised on the one hand as relatively constricted and passive information provision and on the other as moving towards the other end of the spectrum as a more active involvement in pursuing the rights in question, with clients generally favouring the latter model, indeed, finding it difficult to conceptionalise the validity of the first model at all. Parallel divisions can be traced in a range of studies, for example, Bond's evaluation of the Coventry CDP's Hillfields Information and Opinion Centre (1972) found that 'there is an information gap and that centres operating in a style acceptable to the local population can help to bridge this gap,' by becoming the 'focal point of local initiative and action across a whole range of self-help and protest activities',[18] i.e., by moving, as a result of resident involvement, from the first to the second of Butcher's models.

Simpson's study of welfare rights workers within local authority social service departments[19] showed that the majority of statutory welfare rights workers expressed the view that their job involved two functions: to maximise individual clients' uptake of benefits *and* to pressure for the reform of that system itself. This is in line with both Wootton's view of social workers[20] as mediators working for their clients, and Sinfield's expansion of this definition to include investigation and agitation on the client's behalf.[21]

But the notion of 'advocacy' has itself been problematic, containing within it as it does considerable variations of emphasis. For example, reflecting upon the US experience, Kutchins and Kutchins concluded that even 'Advocacy is nothing more than a technique,' and that 'technical innovations are inadequate to remedy the social problems which gave impetus to advocacy in the last fifteen years – poverty, racism and related deprivations.'[22] Even going beyond the neutral provision of information and taking up clients' cases for them was necessary, they considered, but insufficient as a strategy to deal with the causes of poverty and social deprivation. As the Davidoffs explained in the chapter on planning in the same collection of essays, advocacy was seen as a way in which the planning profession, and, in parallel, the legal and social work professions, could give assistance to the client 'by providing information and even advising clients on how to present their own alternative perspectives'. Nevertheless, they argued that the strongest interests still win, however logically the alternative case had been argued. It would appear, therefore, that information and even advocacy assist the disadvantaged primarily in terms of strengthening their leverage. The Davidoffs go on to advocate Alinsky's approach to community organisation, emphasising both the organisation of the client community and their education so as to reduce their dependency upon professionals. Furthermore, even this will be insufficient, they argue, to affect more fundamental disparities of power, so that the poor must also be organised politically, the first minimum step being voter registration.[23]

While the Davidoffs locate themselves clearly within a pluralist perspective on the state, they conclude, nevertheless, that information, advice, even advocacy, per se, are inadequate as strategies to combat poverty, let alone to revitalise democracy. While necessary in themselves, such approaches have to be linked to a wider process of organising at both the community level and at the political level. Left critics of pluralist perspectives, from C. Wright Mills onwards, could be expected to put even greater emphasis upon the necessity to supplement information and advice with support for community education and political education and organisation – moving, in other words, from a technical to a more overtly political conception. As the Davidoffs have also pointed out, the very role of the professional 'advocates' themselves is problematic. At one end of the spectrum, the advisor/expert retains control of his/her expertise; towards the other end of the spectrum, in contrast, there is increasing emphasis on involving the clients and client community and, ultimately, on the necessity for devising mechanisms for sharing expertise and for promoting the development of client autonomy and self-organisation.

The failure of the professions, particularly medicine and the law, to meet the needs of society's poorer members has been a long-established theme in debates about the welfare state. The establishment of the NHS in 1948 and Legal Aid in 1949, together with the Tribunal System can be seen as typifying the more optimistic and technical approach to information and advocacy. Formally speaking, certain crucial professional services were now available, regardless of the means to pay for them.

In contrast, the more critical studies of the welfare state in the sixties recognised that formal access to professional advice and advocacy was demonstrably inadequate. For example, the US Department of Health, Education and Welfare set out the view that legal services would have to be provided in different ways if they were to be relevant to the national fight against poverty; the poor would have to be reached in new ways using new styles of 'aggressive innovative counsel'.[24]

This tougher style of advocacy was itself subject to critical evaluation in the wake of the first thrusts of the welfare rights movement in the US and the development of the poverty lobby in Britain, from the mid sixties. In particular the role of the professional advocate was considered, not simply in relation to the professional effectiveness of various styles of operation in terms of delivering 'the goods' from the relevant welfare agencies for their clients, but also in terms of the effects of the encounter on the clients, in turn. Was the client left in a purely passive role, still individualised and alienated by the whole process? Bell's study of tribunal advocates identified the most appropriate tribunal advocate not at all as an 'impersonal appellant in a purely passive role. Rather he or she was seen as an extension of the appellant, assisting him/her, speaking up for him/her, acting in conjunction with him/her.'[25]

Rose has, similarly, been deeply critical of the 'professional style of certain middle-class advocates, however well-briefed, who retreated with the Tribunal Chairperson into an experts' world, leaving the appellant no longer an actor in his/her own destiny, but merely the object of the case at issue.'[26]

The role of professional was being questioned, not simply in terms of style of formal effectiveness, but in more general terms of client autonomy and democratic accountability. Community Law Centres' attempts to evolve more democratic management structures, directly involving community organisations from their client communities, represent a parallel example of this questioning process about the democratic accountability of professionals in relation to community organisations. Similar questions were being raised within Information and Advice Centres, for example, Bond's argument about the necessity for democratic involvement and accountability in the Hillfields Information and Opinion Centre, if the centre was to operate in a style which was relevant and seen to be relevant by the client community.[27]

It should be emphasised as an aside, at this point, however, that it is the significance of the issue of local involvement and management of information services which is being underlined, not the solutions, which are more problematic. Chapter 3 has already drawn attention to some of the difficulties of operationalising local community management structure in practice.

To summarise, information-giving has to be compared and contrasted not only with advocacy, but with an approach to advocacy which emphasises the significance of resident and client self-organisation, including democratic community management of the information and advocacy services in question. In parallel, the role of the professional, as the Davidoffs outlined, would be viewed in terms of the impartial expert, at one end of the spectrum through that of the more partisan advocate and on to the role of the community educator and the facilitator of self-organisation.

A further parallel would relate these different emphases with varying theoretical assumptions about the nature of the state in Western social democracies; with the more straightforwardly pluralist being associated with information provision and advocacy per se and the left pluralist and beyond, emphasising the additional necessity not only for advocacy but for client self-organisation and for community education, including political education.

Whilst such a model might be appropriate for the purpose of analysis, relating to the necessity but the inherent insufficiency of information provision per se, it could, however, be seriously misleading as an interpretation of the operations of information agencies such as the resource centres, in practice. In reality, and depending upon the presenting case in question, resource centres, in parallel with law centres, for example, have typically offered a range of approaches, usually including individual/group, information and advice-giving and advocacy, as well as offering more collective and community-based forms of intervention and education.

Certain cases may even require some combination of any or all of these components. Similarly, resource centres which have concentrated upon facilitating community self-organisation and education to the *exclusion* of more limited information provision would seem to be exceptional. As the case study from South Wales illustrates, the pressures for individual casework have been powerful indeed. In practice, then, the key question is not so much to ask where any particular service or activity would locate its host project/resource centre, but rather to ask how, if at all, the range of project/centre activities interact, and where the limits are defined. Is information provision creatively related to other project interventions, whether in advocacy or community organisation, and how or why does the agency/resource centre define the proper limits to its information-providing role?

The case studies which are the subject of the rest of this chapter deal with different ends of the spectrum, from the publication of a newsletter, at one end, to the provision of welfare rights training and support for local community organisation around welfare rights issues at the other. As it will be argued subsequently, however, in each case the project activities, in fact, related to an overall resource centre strategy which included elements more obviously categorised as falling at the opposite end of the spectrum. So, the newsletter was related to and supportive of community organisation activities, while the welfare rights project was backed up by access to the resource centre's lawyer who was available for consultation on individual cases. It was these interactions which became a key focus for the evaluation process.

The CWS newsletter

The CWS team themselves explained the significance of the newsletter in their overall strategy, in relation to the size and complexity of their constituency requiring an information service in London. The sheer size of London's population and its geographical spread would have been, they considered, problematic enough for the eight workers of the CWS. Furthermore, community groups were relatively highly developed, so that client organisations themselves represented a significant, although geographically disparate, constituency.

Support services for community groups were correspondingly complex. As the CWS team explained, within London there were upwards of 1,000-2,000 community 'agencies' with a brief which could be considered as 'community work', i.e., the agency was charged with the task of developing autonomous local groupings of people who were organising around a particular issue, whether it be to provide or improve services, influence some question of social policy such as housing or education in their area, or some other matter which affected the lives of their members.

These 'agencies', which included some community work component, covered an enormous variety of resources, ranging from the area-based 'community worker', within the Social Services Department of a London borough (perhaps servicing, with one community worker, an area with a population of around 20,000 people), through to independent local advice centres, law centres, settlements, councils for voluntary service, social action centres, workers with mothers and preschool children, community relations councils, and community health councils. The distribution of these agencies was uneven across the city, but tended to relate to the degree of community organisation achieved within the local area (both as cause and effect).

Overall, CWS's strategy involved working through these 'second tier' agencies, to achieve an adequate spread of contacts and support points throughout the city. These contact points would be supplied with, as well as themselves supplying, information, the aim being to trigger off a process involving the cross-fertilisation of information and the exchange of experiences, with the ultimate goal of benefiting not only the agency but their client groups and local populations, more generally.

Even this process of operating indirectly through a second tier of community work agencies involved very considerable numbers, however, some 10,000 individuals and contact points perhaps, in the 1,000 relevant agencies. So CWS decided that, in addition to the other activities of the service, the unit would establish a regular vehicle of communication between itself and the community agencies' activities within the wider London constituency. The resulting end-product was the regular publication of the 'London Community Work Service Newsletter', which was circulated to around 1,000 community agencies throughout London, eleven times a year To summarise, then, the newsletter fitted into the CWS strategy in a number of ways, both as a means of communication itself and as a support for community work and community action.

More specifically, CWS aimed not only to provide information and support at a metropolitan level, but also to provide information and support to community groups, in as much as they were themselves affected by metropolitan, as opposed to strictly local, issues. For although there were several hundreds of community groups within London concerned with a vast number of local issues, few were concerned with metropolitan policies per se, CWS believed, even though these metropolitan policies affected their activities and the likelihood of their achieving their aims (just as, in parallel, and increasingly overtly, the policies of national government set the wider context and the consequent constraints upon their demands).

In community work terms, 'London' was at that time, CWS felt, barely visible (although subsequent changes in policies since the election of the Labour GLC in 1981 may be having a considerable effect on this situation for the future). But in the late seventies the funding of community work and community activities within London, for example, was for the most part undertaken at the level of the thirty-two borough councils. When combined with the fact that borough councils were the major providers of the services and the formulators of the policies that community groups were typically most actively concerned with (such as housing, social services and provision for pre-school children), it was not surprising, CWS believed, that the major pressure points which many groups were trying to influence were themselves relatively local (although, in practice an agency such as a London borough covering some 200,000 people could still seem sufficiently remote to the groups and individuals concerned). So there was, CWS considered, both a psychological and a structural gap between organising around issues at borough level (where people tended to know members of the other community groups 'on the local network'), and at a metropolitan level. As a result, similar types of community organisations were wrestling with comparable problems in adjacent boroughs with little or no knowledge of each other's existence, let alone of each other's experiences. The attempt to tackle this problem of fragmentation was a major goal, both for the newsletter, specifically, and for the CWS service, more generally.

One of the prime, concrete tasks which CWS set for the newsletter was to provide those working with community organisations with information about key metropolitan agencies (such as the Greater London Council, Inner London Education Authority and London Transport), the policies which they were pursuing, and the effects of those policies at local level. (In retrospect, this analysis of the situation represents a point of comparison and contrast, since the London-wide level of community organising, for example around transport, became so much more evident under the Labour-controlled GLC in 1981.)

Meanwhile back in the late seventies, despite the constraints of resources for the newsletter which limited the realisation of these aims, issues such as the problem of London Transport and the transfer of GLC housing estates to the boroughs (together with the local impact of that policy) were treated fully in the newsletter, in contrast with the relatively sparse coverage of these issues in other community work publications and local community newspapers.

The newsletter was also considered central to the work of the metropolitan resource centre in a number of other specific ways, such as for publicising meetings and campaigns organised through the support of CWS itself, alongside publicity for community groups' meetings and campaigning activities more generally. This link between the newsletter's role as a provider of information and as a support for associated activities can be traced, for example, in relation to its coverage of proposed changes in urban aid. The newsletter carried a long article, explaining these proposed developments within the urban programme, together with the announcement of a meeting of interested parties which led to further campaigning activity, and this in turn was reflected in the newsletter's own coverage.

Initially, the newsletter was mailed off to those agencies, organisations and individuals whom CWS estimated to be potentially in need of the service. Then, at the beginning of 1979, the team decided to test how far their readers were really concerned to receive this newsletter. The recipients were informed that they would no longer automatically be kept on the mailing list. In future, only those readers who took the initiative in asking for it would continue to receive copies. Within a couple of months over half the initial readership had responded positively and by the end of the year the readership was well over the initial circulation level. This explicit demand for the newsletter did seem to indicate, then, that some value was being placed upon its regular arrival. So the fact that this readership for the newsletter did exist was some confirmation of CWS's starting assumptions; but crucial questions remained. There was no formal feed-back about the balance of the newsletter's coverage, and in particular there were no means of knowing whether or not the information which it conveyed bore any systematic relation to the require-ments of community organisations and activists in practice.

The next phase of the evaluation was a survey of a random sample of newsletter recipients, to elicit their views on coverage in general and the newsletter's relevance or lack of relevance for their practice. In the event, the survey was a pilot, partly because there was considerable and, as it turned out, unjustified scepticism about the feasibility of conducting the survey by post (in fact, three-quarters of those originally mailed did respond, with relatively little prompting, so that it did not prove necessary to interview them in person). Although the numbers were too small for detailed analysis, certain trends did emerge quite clearly from the replies.

Overall, the newsletter was seen in a very positive light – over 90 per cent said that they found it useful or 'very useful'. The overwhelming majority also shared the newsletter's contents with at least one, and typically with several, colleagues or fellow members of their organisation.

In terms of coverage, the readers were asked to comment both in terms of past issues and in terms of the topics which they would like to be covered in future issues. In each case a relatively clear and consistent pattern emerged.

The most frequently mentioned topics which readers remembered were fairly general ones – 'meetings and activities relevant to community work in London', and 'campaigns against closures or redevelopment plans', closely followed by 'information on voluntary projects' and 'fighting the cuts'. These combinations of general community work information and campaigning news seemed to predominate.

In addition, the more specific topics (of education, health and housing, for example) were each mentioned by a quarter of the readers. Once again, too, there was emphasis upon these topics in relation to community organisation and action. In particular, readers tended to over-emphasise the coverage of these topics in terms of the public expenditure cuts and cuts campaigns (as compared with a content's analysis of the most recent issues of the newsletter). The best-remembered topics, then, were those which related most closely to practice, and specifically to community action campaigns.

A similar pattern emerged in terms of the value which the readers placed upon the coverage of these different topics. Over half the readers made special mention of the usefulness of the newsletter's coverage of community work in London in general, and campaigning news in particular. In addition, a third singled out the information about 'the cuts' as being crucial. A clearly identified readership for more specialised articles on topics such as housing/planning, education, health, welfare rights, and race relations also emerged.

Overall, though, it was the general spread of news and information about community work, community action and broad campaigning work which constituted the newsletter's clearest appeal. In addition, half the readers referred to some specific ways in which they had used information from the newsletter in their own practice.

In terms of the newsletter's future coverage, a third simply commented that they hoped it would continue in the same way and a further third said that they wanted plenty of news of other projects' work and/or a broad range of topics (i.e., a similar coverage to the present one). A smaller number asked for more background information on relevant national policy changes, while even smaller numbers asked for more coverage on their own particular areas of interest (such as housing and education). When these more specialised replies were examined in relation to the replies to previous questions, it emerged that it was indeed the same readers, in many cases, who kept referring to each of these, more specific, topics (i.e., their own particular spheres of interest). Once again, this would seem to reinforce the view that the readers were typically using the newsletter as a support service for their own practice; and conversely and not at all surprisingly, there seemed to be little if any interest in information per se.

This general impression was confirmed by the tenor of the replies about the newsletter's style of presentation and lay-out. There was considerable emphasis upon the value of a factual and practical presentation; very few readers wanted the newsletter to be either more theoretical on the one hand, or more popular and amusing on the other. Nor did the overwhelming majority want the newsletter to be more overtly didactic, or political in its editorial style. While the issues of most concern to the majority of the readers *were* clearly political in their implications, it seemed that they felt no need to have these political implications spelt out for them through some editorial 'line'.

Part of the explanation for this widespread attitude may have been that all but one of the readers said that they were regular readers of at least one other paper or journal which commented upon comparable issues (for example, *Community Action* and *New Society*, as well as party-political periodicals). In general, then, the readers were already highly conscious of their information needs, and, typically, also regularly in touch with a range of commentaries including overtly political commentaries on relevant issues.

So why did they read the CWS newsletter as well? As one reader explained, he could find some or even much of the information which it contained from other sources, but the newsletter put these disparate sources of information together in a relevant combination. It was also valued for being 'easy to read, short and well written'.

Finally, and most importantly, the newsletter was valued as a contact point, not just for contacts with other community or campaigning organisations but for the contact which it provided with CWS itself. The newsletter and the frequent enclosures containing further information on particular topics including CWS's own training programme were, as one reader commented, a regular 'reminder that CWS is there as a source of a wide range of information.'

To summarise, the pilot survey did seem to bear out the CWS team's justification for the newsletter as a key element in their overall strategy. Its value was directly proportionate to its two-way relationship with practice, gathering information on community work and community action in London, and then reporting back these experiences to stimulate the wider constituency in turn.

In general, the most enthusiastic readers of the newsletter were those who seemed to be most directly involved in community action and the Labour movement, and these were the readers most likely to share their copies with the largest number of their colleagues. These readers were also typically extremely practical; they wanted contact names, addresses and phone numbers, rather than simply accounts of good community work practice, or even successful campaigning per se.

Information provision was, then, only one of the functions of the CWS newsletter. As the team members themselves had already identified, information was valued by the typical reader but in direct proportion to its practical relevance for organisation and action.

The newly elected Labour GLC accepted this interpretation of the relevance of the newsletter as a resource for community action at metropolitan level when they agreed to fund its continued existence in 1981.

The CWS training sessions on health and community work

An illustration of CWS training work, in relation to CWS information work more generally

The CWS training programme was a key element, too, in their overall strategy, and in some senses a specialised aspect of their information strategy. The newsletter covered announcements of training events, and periodic enclosures offered details of courses and conferences of possible interest to community workers and community groups in London. Education and training were defined broadly to include not only formal programmes and information provision, but more informal sessions too. As CWS's report to ILEA 1979/80 explained, this was part of CWS's overall strategy to break down the isolation of so many community groups and to support the development of links between them through spreading 'ideas and information' and 'ensuring that community projects can benefit by one another's knowledge and experiences rather than each have to learn by their own mistakes.'[28]

In general, CWS only organised courses and sessions directly themselves when they felt that they were identifying a gap in existing provision, where new developments in the field were not being met by the present training opportunities. These CWS courses were intended, then, as pioneering ventures, both in terms of training and in terms of community work and community action: to share experience and to support practice in developing areas of work – the relationship, once again, between providing information and stimulating organisation and practice.

The health training sessions illustrated all those aspects. CWS's awareness of the increase in community health struggles in London can be traced through the newsletter's expanding coverage of the growing interest in community work in this field. As the CWS paper 'Community health work in the Inner City: the London experience' explained:

> over the last few years the women's movement, the unionis-ation of hospital and health workers, the re-organisations and cutbacks in the National Health Service, the creation of community health councils and the radical movements in the health service itself have been important forces in creating a new awareness that health and illness are important issues for public and collective concern. The resultant community activity is most clearly seen in several community health projects in London.

These projects' activities 'reflect a recognition of the relationships between social class, poverty and health, and the inequalities in health care provisions that exist between deprived and more affluent areas'. The increasing unionisation of public sector workers, including health workers, was another strand which was part of the developing trade union concern. Joint trade union and community action was clearly increasingly on the political agenda:[29]

> The London CWS's involvement in this field has been growing
> steadily over the last few years. . . . The main aim of our
> involvement is . . . to bring together the wealth of experience
> that is emerging on the ground.

To explore the possibilities of sharing these experiences, an afternoon seminar was arranged as a once-off event, initially, and publicised, evidently effectively, through the newsletter in April 1979. At this session, as the 1978/79 report explained: 'The subject really captured the imagination of workers. Thirty-two attended and there was a real level of interest and enthusiasm.'[30] As a result, the group asked CWS to 'run regular sessions on community health topics'.

These seminars were, then, a direct response to demands expressed by community workers, community groups and health workers. There was a series of nine community health seminars for those with some prior involvement and interest in community health work and, in addition, a course of five introductory sessions on community health for those whose interest in this subject was only just developing. These sessions included projects' experience of community health work, women's health groups, the relationship between health and housing, and the politics of health. The short course also covered the cuts in the NHS and what could be done to fight them.

In addition to the general feedback which CWS received in terms of the demand for further sessions, a small sample of those who had attended filled in questionnaires afterwards, as part of the evaluation process. From this it emerged that three-quarters had come either because they were already involved in health issues and wanted to share their experiences and extend their knowledge, or because they had plans to become involved in the near future, and wanted to prepare for this: 'I came for support, ideas and to share experiences of health work,' said one. 'Partly for my own education, and partly to make contact with other people and to compare their experiences with my own,' commented another.

The comments on each specific session were almost exclusively positive to enthusiastic. The positive comments included the following: 'This session helped me to get the feel of the links between community work and community health;' 'they were very useful as a starting point for me, in developing community health work.' There were more specific comments on particular sessions, too: 'The sessions on the NHS and the CHCs seemed to make clear the complex levels of these organisations. The cuts session was informative because it helped me find out what other areas were doing and which organisations were involved.'

Subsequently in the questionnaire, the participants were asked more specifically to comment upon how, if at all, the sessions had affected their practice. Only one replied that the sessions had made no difference, although a small minority did not answer this question at all. The positive answers referred to gaining greater knowledge and awareness of health issues and how community groups could tackle them. One attributed the launching of a community health project to the workers' attendance at the sessions. Other positive features included the informal contacts and opportunities to share experiences.

These comments included the following views on the value of the informal discussions:

'They helped me in clarifying where I was going and where I might go in the future.'

'They provided useful contacts, knowledge of what others were doing and ideas for future developments.'

'The discussions helped me to get a realistic perspective for my own work.'

'It was useful to pick up other people's ideas and to use others as a sounding board to refine your plans. It is supportive just to know that you are not the only one hacking away.'

On the whole, those who were already involved in health work were the most positive in their comments, and the most likely to offer enthusiastic comments about the need for further training sessions. Once again, information and training were being valued, it seemed, in direct relation to the support which they offered for practice.

The community health training example was significant, too, in terms of illustrating the links between CWS's information work and its own overall follow-up strategy. Having confirmed their identification of health as such a rapidly developing area of interest, CWS decided to pursue this by establishing a specific support service for community health work in London. A proposal was drawn up for a separate community health resource centre, staffed by workers with a primary responsibility for health development work. This was to encompass the building of a London community health information resource unit and library, and further work with CHCs, health educationalists, community health personnel, and other groupings of relevance to community workers and community groups more generally. This community health centre was also to work with CRCs to promote work on health and race. In addition, the centre would provide for the further development of the current health training work.

A development such as this would, it was argued, free CWS as a generalist resource centre from the risk of stressing the newly developing area of health at the expense of other areas of community work and community action, because of the expressed needs in the field. More positively, it would enable a wider and more thorough exploration of the potential of community health work to be carried out than would be possible within the limitations of a more generalist area resource centre, such as CWS. The new centre could also develop closer links with its more specific constituency in terms of participation and democratic accountability. Funding was obtained for this community health resource unit to be established, early in 1981.

SWAPAC's tribunal access unit (TAU)

The TAU project was concerned to develop the local working-class community's own information base, expertise and capacity to take up welfare rights problems, to provide effective representation for its own members, and to organise around these issues.

Claimants or former claimants were the prime target group for the volunteer advocates' training courses, together with 'those key residents who were informally looked to for advice and guidance by their fellow residents'.

TAU set out to identify these local contact points, and to support them by providing them with the expertise which could help them to be more effective in the role which they were already performing. The aim was to build upon the strengths of the local working-class communities, and to develop their collective expertise and support networks, rather than simply to provide them with welfare rights information or even with an effective professional advocacy service.

Even so, these latter services did still have to be provided; as it has already been suggested earlier in this chapter, the demand for immediate and more individualised support services was inevitably pressing and TAU did spend far more time than it had originally planned on the provision of individual information and advocacy. Had the project been more adequately resourced it might have been easier to achieve the balance which had first been envisaged. Ironically, it was only at the end of TAU's funding that local groups did actually come together to form the broader organisation which had been the original aim. Before attempting to evaluate the TAU experience in detail, however, it will be necessary to summarise the project's rationale, structure and specific mode of operation.

The continuing and growing need for tribunal representation systems

Administrative tribunals were originally set up in the anticipation that they would be directly accessible to the ordinary public. Unlike the formal courts, justice would not depend on securing the services of a professional lawyer. Tribunals would be less formal and more comprehensive so that the appellant would simply present his or her own case, without fear of prejudicing the outcome through lack of legal knowledge of skills in advocacy. But, in practice, as SWAPAC argued, this expectation has not been fulfilled. On the contrary, the current system of tribunals has been operating with an in-built bias against unrepresented clients. For example, in 1976, when the Tribunal Access Unit was being planned, only 13 per cent of unrepresented clients won their supplementary benefit appeals, as contrasted with 50 per cent of the clients represented by social workers and 44.6 per cent of cases represented by a trade union or claimants union – and as the number of appeals grew, these differences were increasing.[31]

So, the unrepresented client has been clearly disadvantaged, and the problem of equity which this situation represents has been growing. The current increase in the number of those unemployed as a result of the combined effects of the recession and the industrial rationalisation process, inevitably increases the number of claimants and so of appellants still further (despite the contrary effects of the decrease in discretion resulting from legislative changes).[32]

Yet, government financial support for agencies operating in the tribunal field and for innovative projects has been increasingly hard to come by, as a result of the limits upon public expenditure, with the result that there has inevitably been increasing emphasis upon utilising voluntary effort. This was becoming widely recognised when the TAU concept was developed. Zander commented, for example, 'The present tide is running strongly in favour of more and better lay advocacy . . . there is plainly a need for some method to fund, out of public monies, and to develop a national system of tribunal advocates.'[33]

The use of volunteers as advocates was not seen as simply a question of financial expediency. On the contrary, the TAU project was planned around the positive advantages of involving lay people to de-mystify the law, making it generally easier for people to understand both their own rights and the legal system itself. Even if solicitors had been widely interested in expanding into tribunal work (which they were not, nor were they particularly competent at it), they would have been less concerned to involve the client in this way. Typically it has taken the involvement of non-professionals to involve the client rather than taking over the case completely leaving him or her in a purely passive role. (This brings the argument to the criticisms which Rose, for example, has made of 'the well-briefed middle-class advocate, retreating with the tribunal chairperson into an expert's world, reinforcing the clients' own powerlessness, and the individualisation of his or her own case.')

The TAU experiment was set up to construct an alternative

model of tribunal representation, using the findings of the claimants' union's experience, for example, and building upon the strengths of the local communities concerned to develop collective expertise and support networks.

The South Wales mining valleys were seen as a particularly appropriate setting for such an experiment, because of the absence of those 'fringe' advice agencies, such as welfare rights groups, which have tended to be available to tribunal appellants in metropolitan areas and university towns. These alternative advice agencies were simply not available. But the area had other strengths: the reservoir of potential representation within the local working-class communities and their community organisations. And, as unemployment increased, representation could offer a socially valuable outlet for the energies and enthusiasm of some of these local people as they became unemployed themselves.

The use of local working-class volunteers became, then, a positive and novel feature in TAU. The emphasis was upon moving from information and advocacy, for the individual client, towards a more collective approach to welfare rights, involving a process of community education, for local residents both in terms of information and in terms of organisation.

The TAU project was eventually established as part of SWAPAC, but with a separate grant from the Nuffield Foundation. There were two project workers, initially working part-time only. John, who had long been active in community affairs, was largely chosen for his insight into the structure and workings of the Welsh Valley communities in which the unit would be mainly operating, and for his excellent local contacts. He had no previous experience of tribunal work. Terry, on the other hand, had been heavily involved for ten years with claimants' unions, advising, teaching and representing tribunal appellants. Both had been unemployed for some time prior to appointment and accordingly had direct personal experience of negotiating the social security system.

For the first year of the project, John and Terry were employed for three and four days per week respectively. A supplementary grant from SWAPAC enabled both of them to be employed full-time during the second year. The project started in September 1977.

The advisory and information service

The first task of the unit, before even embarking upon identifying and training local volunteers, was to establish an advisory and information service on tribunals and tribunal representation. This was also an opportunity for the members of the unit to familiarise themselves with those tribunals of which they had insufficient experience.

This was an essential process, because of the extent to which tribunals differ. They do not have the same form of composition, the same practice or procedure. Most importantly, they do not apply the same substantive law. So, techniques of advocacy or other skills that may be applied generically to tribunals are few. It would be impossible, for example, to offer training in tribunal representation for supplementary benefit appeal tribunals without providing a sound working knowledge of social security. Nor would it be reasonable to expect someone versed in supplementary benefit appeal tribunals to feel equally at home before a mental health review tribunal.

So, the Tribunal Access Unit did not set out to deal with all of the fifty or more species of tribunal under the general supervision of the Council on Tribunals, each with its own peculiar and daunting body of law. The unit would establish priorities, taking into account factors such as the demand for assistance by category of tribunal, the particular skills and expertise that the unit's workers brought to their jobs, the availability of assistance to appellants from other sources, and the complexity of legal or other technical argument or practice likely to be encountered during the process of problem-resolution.

So, at this stage, what was hoped to be a manageable number of tribunals was selected. The tribunals which were eventually chosen were as follows:

(i) *Supplementary Benefit Appeal Tribunals* – chosen for their large actual and potential caseload, their simplicity of law and procedure, and the existing experience of the unit's workers.

(ii) *National Insurance Local Tribunals* – chosen for caseload as before, and the existing experience of the unit's workers.

(iii) *Mental Health Review Tribunals* – chosen for the importance of their determinations (the liberty of the patient), the lack of other agencies, and the scope for lay representation because of the dual role of the representative as advocate and 'fixer', i.e., arranging jobs, accommodation and suchlike which have an important influence on the outcome of the appeal.

(iv) *Lands Tribunals* – chosen for the significance of its leasehold enfranchisement jurisdiction in South Wales and for the scope of collective lay involvement.

(v) *Industrial Tribunals* – chosen for their caseload as before.

Compiling information

There was no central repository of material giving the hard practical information required by the unit for its work on tribunals. Consequently, the unit had to make a wide-ranging inquiry both of official bodies and voluntary agencies to discover what relevant material actually existed. At a local level, much of the information required was found to be unrecorded – being locked up in the personal experience of those already involved in the field.

Within these limitations, the unit set about collecting the following kinds of information:

(i) Manuals of law and practice
(ii) Eye-witness accounts
(iii) Personal accounts

Statutes, statutory regulations and legal textbooks setting out the substantive law administered by the tribunals were already available in SWAPAC's library. The manuals sought by the unit were a blend of law, practice and procedure, presented in a way that would be readily intelligible to the layperson, and, accordingly, suitable for use as course material in the training programme. The most useful works of this nature, TAU found, were produced by groups like CPAG and MIND.

This formal information was only part of the unit's information bank, however. An appellant can be as flustered, and the appeal jeopardised, in consequence, by the attitude of a tribunal chairperson or by the lay-out of the tribunal room as by ignorance of the law itself. But systematic information of this sort usually lies outside the scope of published works, even such information as may be available is often vitiated by local idiosyncratic variations from nationally recommended practice.

So, the unit endeavoured to build up its own eye-witness accounts of the reality of local tribunal hearings (and the incidental stages of problem-resolution) by attending and conducting appeals before supplementary benefit tribunals, national insurance local tribunals and industrial tribunals. The anecdotal information gleaned in this way may be short-lived and often scurrilous, but it is, in fact, invaluable to appellants. Unfortunately, it did not prove practicable to put these impressions of tribunals 'in the raw' into recorded form for wider dissemination, simply because they were so specific in their application. They could, however, be readily fed into the unit's own training programme.

One other important point should be mentioned here: manuals describe expected behaviour and tend not to offer contingent advice. For example, appellants to national insurance local tribunals are told that they can obtain access to reports of commissioner's decisions, for use as precedents, at social security offices. They are not warned how to deal with the obstructive reactions which are all too frequently encountered on making a request for access. Manuals alone cannot instil the self-confidence needed to cope with such situations.

The advice service

Once a suitable bank of information had been acquired by the unit, the existence of the advice service was publicised by a circular issued to local social service departments, community centres, Citizens' Advice Bureaux and other formal points of contact with potential tribunal appellants. Initially, inquiries were to be limited to supplementary benefit appeal tribunals and national insurance local tribunals only. As anticipated however the questions and requests for assistance which were received were not limited to tribunals and tribunal procedure, but covered the whole range of welfare rights.

So, the initial advice and information bank service was

extended to include the provision of talks and seminars on welfare rights. Although these talks touched upon tribunals, they were not designed as courses of training in tribunal representation, but represented a contribution to the more basic work of stimulating interest in the system of social security more generally. In this sense, such talks formed part of the process of increasing awareness, so that claimants could be in a position to realise that they may have a case, in the first place.

As the unit moved into the next phase of its operation, namely the training itself, it was decided to concentrate upon supplementary benefit appeal tribunals and national insurance local tribunals. Mental health review tribunals and lands tribunals were dropped for practical problems, and industrial tribunals were accorded low priority because of the great time-burden which these placed upon the volunteers, and because trade union officials were already providing representation in this field.

The training programme

While the key target-group for volunteers was the local community itself, some professionals were also reached by the TAU training programme. For example, social workers from three local Social Services Departments attended courses (although acting upon their own initiative rather than their department's official concern with welfare rights issues). Social workers did also refer cases, and similarly cooperative relationships were established with local solicitors in terms of referrals.

Local organisations and claimants themselves represented the major focus, however. A profile of the first trainees illustrates the range of these local activists:

Mr C. – in his 60s, long-term unemployed, heavily involved in a voluntary capacity with a local community centre where he was regularly approached for advice.

Mr W. – in his 60s, long-term unemployed, vast experience from pursuing his own claims to benefit.

Mr P. – in his 50s, retired through disablement, claimant.

Mrs R. – pensioner, claimant.

Mr S. – in his 50s, long-term invalidity claimant.

Mr. G. – in his 30s, community councillor, then shortly to go on a community work course.

Mr J. – in his 60s, long-term invalidity claimant.

Five of the trainees came from a mining village in the Rhondda Valley. The other two were from a council estate on the edge of a market town. Some had handled tribunal work before, but generally only in the capacity of 'holding the appellant's hand'. Some had formerly held trade union office and hence had experience of handling disputes. None had received training of any sort in social security law.

Each course was organised with a distinctive flavour, as the unit soon discovered that relatively homogenous groupings were the most successful for training purposes. For example, one group was predominantly made up of single mothers, another of pensioners. While each course took into account the particular interests of the trainees, however, there was a common core of the following:

    (i) an opening talk provided an overview of the social security system and placed tribunals in a wider context of problem resolution;

  (ii) the successive stages of handling a social security problem were explained in detail, using taped interviews and sample papers;

 (iii) the tribunal hearing was described and two video films of mock hearings shown to illustrate different styles of advocacy;

 (iv) a general discussion was held on the nature of social security with opportunities for the trainees to bring out their own experiences;

  (v) arrangements were made for trainees to obtain further experience through, for example, sitting in on tribunals as observers, and encouragement was given to the group forming a tribunal 'sub-unit'.

Each course involved both the unit's workers and lasted two days (10 am-5 pm). Trainees were usually set a homework problem, say, drafting an appeal letter, after the end of the first day's session.

Through the course of follow-up support, TAU was intended to develop the knowledge, skills and organisations of the local community. TAU originally planned to represent individual cases itself only in the following cases:

(i) cases taken initially to build up the experience of the unit's workers and to establish the reputation of the unit;

(ii) cases taken from time to time to keep the unit up-to-date with current tribunal procedure;

(iii) cases taken in conjunction with trainees as practical instruction;

(iv) cases of particular complexity referred by trainees.

But once the unit began to take on work under category (i), it became exceedingly difficult to call a halt and the unit entered a spiral in which pressure of casework precluded it from organising training courses, when training courses and hence trainees were the only means to satisfy the pressure of casework. The expectation, originally held, that the non-central location of the unit's premises would be an effective control on casework demands proved misguided, as claimants struggled to Merthyr, from as far as 35 miles away, in a desperate search for assistance.

Although the training programme, the prime function of the project, was being endangered by casework demands, the unit's workers naturally found it exceedingly difficult to turn away anyone in need, knowing that there was no one else who could help. Demands increased as word of the assistance provided by the unit spread quickly on the claimants' grapevine.

Due to the understandable reluctance of the unit's workers to reject calls for help and the difficulty, once the precedent had been set, of providing representation to some claimants but not others, ways of introducing organisational forms of rationing were discussed; for example, limiting the case-work service to particular sections of claimants, say, pensioners. The unit would then only be held out as available to that section. This proposal was rejected on the ground that it would be invidious to mark out one section of claimants as somehow more deserving of assistance than others.

Redrawing the boundaries of the unit's area of operation was not feasible, either, as there was sufficient casework demand in Merthyr alone (with population of 60,000) to impose a strain on the unit, and retiring from the rest of the region would forfeit the interest in attending training courses, which had already been generated there.

The demand was reduced to more manageable proportions eventually by refusing referrals from agencies such as social service departments, which could be expected themselves to provide some, even if not sufficient, assistance to the claimant.

In all, the unit itself provided representation at forty-four appeal hearings. A further eleven appeals were settled without hearings. Not the least significant of these cases was the success rate before supplementary benefit appeals tribunals of 79 per cent, which shows, in no uncertain terms, the value of representation. Many more cases were brought to a conclusion in the client's favour without recourse to a formal appeal. However successful, though, this individual case work was not the original focus of TAU, and the pressures to take up individual cases were a source of tension between that and the training work.

The trainees themselves

On 'graduating' from a course, each trainee was provided with manuals, leaflets and other material, and arrangements were made for them to sit in on central tribunals as observers. The graduate was then considered 'fully fledged' and ready to take up referrals, although in practice of course the 'graduate' was already dealing with a range of cases in his/her capacity as informal advisor in the local community.

In principle, the 'graduates' were supposed to make regular returns of the cases which they took up, so that TAU could monitor their progress and offer follow-up support if and when necessary. In practice, however, quite understandably this did not take place on a systematic basis. Many 'graduates' were far too busy taking up cases to bother with form-filling. Nor did every trainee go on to take up representation, although this did not necessarily mean that none of their newly acquired knowledge and understanding filtered through to their friends and relatives.

TAU did try to support local groups of former trainees, although the pressure of providing training and taking up individual cases restricted the time which they could put into this crucial aspect of the project. Not surprisingly, then, a firm organisation in terms of a federation of volunteers' groups only developed in the latter phase of the project. The links and yet the tensions between the pressure for advice and advocacy on an individual basis and the goal of community education and organisation on the other provided, then, a recurrent theme.

The views of the trainee volunteers and their clients

So far, we have concentrated upon the TAU concept and the project's formal achievements. How successful were the trainee volunteers, themselves, and what did their clients believe the project's distinctive approach to be?

Early in 1980, a sample survey of some fifty volunteers, clients, and tribunal members was carried out, as part of the evaluation of TAU. These interviews provided the material on which this section is based.

The trainees emerged from the interviews as typical of the different types of potential volunteer which TAU had already identified (i.e., relevant professionals such as social workers, local politicians, claimants themselves and informal advisors who already played key roles in their local communities).

Despite these differences, the volunteers did also share a number of common personal characteristics, being typical of the range of the more organised and vocal sections of the local population. Although they included two with professional occupations, for example, in general, the volunteers still seemed relatively close, rather than distanced from the life-experiences of their potential clients. This relates back to TAU's original aims of using lay representatives to 'bridge the gap, de-mystify the law, and making it generally easier for people to understand both their own rights and the legal system itself'. For example, even one of those with professional qualifications had himself experienced being a claimant. In terms of membership of local organisations, there were no apparent differences between the community councillors, for instance, and the other volunteers. In fact, only one volunteer was not a member of at least one organisation, such as a community association or a trade union branch; other organisations included youth clubs (as organisers), Women's Aid,

Gingerbread and choirs. Thus the range included examples of both the more traditional and the more recently established issue-orientated organisations of the area. Some had initially become involved in a TAU training course, because they hoped it would help them to be more effective in their present roles (the community councillor, for instance); others became involved in welfare rights work through their own experiences as a claimant.

Overall, the volunteers felt very positive about their training experience, both in terms of what they had learnt about welfare rights and in terms of learning how to cope with the tribunal situation itself. There was also some recognition that, however well-organised a training course might be, ultimately it can be no substitute for experience. As one volunteer commented: 'Yes, the training was adequate. But training can only give a core of knowledge which has to be developed through experience.'

The volunteers were also agreed on their commitment to working with their clients on the basis of a partnership. The ideal was for the case to be prepared jointly, involving the client at every step. The volunteers were realistic, however, about the fact that this was often difficult to achieve, especially if there was very little time to prepare the case, or if the client was elderly and housebound, for example. But the client's involvement and understanding were seen as very important issues. 'We are working on this,' said one, 'even if we have to drum the issues into them.' Part of this problem of maximising the clients' understanding arose, it was felt, from the DHSS's own practices, and from tribunals' failures to offer reasons for the rejection of particular appeals.

Towards the end of the interviews, the volunteers were asked for their comments and suggestions for improving TAU services. The majority view was that the service should be extended, with more resources, more advocates and greater publicity: 'More groups are needed . . . the strength of TAU is that advocates have their roots in their own highly localised community – this should be developed.' Other suggestions included more training, and more reference books for back-up support. In general, then, the volunteers felt that there should be more of the same service, extended to meet the needs of a wider range of local people.

Finally, the volunteers were asked what they felt would be the effect on the local community if the TAU service was no longer available. There was widespread concern. It would be a 'tragic loss', said one. 'The *one* source of help available locally for claimants would disappear. The potential for developing a community-based network of advocates would no longer exist,' said another. 'The long-term effects could be devastating,' said another.

Were their clients as positive about the contribution which the TAU project was making? Overall, they were.

Firstly, the survey fully confirmed the relevance of using local people as volunteers. Clients expressed all sorts of reservations about getting advice from traditional (and more middle-class based) volunteer agencies such as the CAB, preferring to confide in someone from their local community: 'I feel more able to talk freely with someone from the community,' said one. 'It is important to talk with someone you know,' said another. 'I treat them [the TAU volunteers] as friends,' commented a third. Other comments emphasised the need to talk to someone you could trust, and the particular value of talking to someone who really understood the problem: 'It is important to have someone with an *understanding* of the problem, i.e., a local person.' 'You can talk to people in a similar situation,' added another respondent. These comments are, of course, in line with Bell's conclusion about the ideal representative.

There were also a number of responses which indicated negative attitudes towards professionals, including professionals such as social workers, with whom the clients might have had more contact. In some cases clients referred to their own personal experiences in relation to these comments: 'I get all wound up when talking to any professional,' commented one respondent. 'I wouldn't talk to a social worker or welfare officer,' said another. 'Once you call them in, they keep coming back.' 'I call them the SS,' commented a third, when explaining why she would not go to social services for help. In both these examples, social services were clearly associated with notions of social control. An alternative criticism which emerged in two other instances was that social workers did not have the time or the expertise to take up welfare rights cases properly.

The clients were all asked to provide a general description of the way in which the TAU representative had handled their case including the extent of the clients' own involvement in the process.

They were specifically asked to comment upon how far they felt that TAU had handled the case for them and how far they themselves had helped to prepare and present the case.

The majority gave answers which clearly indicated that there had been a partnership between themselves and TAU; TAU had helped them to prepare their case and to present it in the most effective way: 'They sorted it out and told me what would happen. They didn't say "do this" or "do that" – we talked it over and worked things out together.' 'We went through it together,' commented another. 'We just took the case step by step and went through the procedure and the issues involved,' said a third. On the other hand, a minority did feel that TAU had essentially done all the preparation and presentation for them; but, in some cases at least, the clients indicated this was how they felt that their cases should have been handled: 'I was happy to leave it to him [the advocate],' commented one housebound old lady, for example. At the other end of the spectrum, one client felt that he or she had basically prepared the case and had enjoyed TAU support only at the tribunal stage.

A majority of clients also considered that they were now better informed about welfare rights and tribunal procedures as a result of their involvement with TAU: 'Jim put me in the picture,' said one. 'Yes, I picked up information through the case,' commented another. 'I've got a little more idea now, at least of what you're entitled to.' In addition, a few commented that although they did not themselves know more about the subject of welfare rights, they would at least know how to find help on another occasion. Only a small minority felt that they had not learned anything about welfare rights, or tribunal procedures.

Clients were also specifically asked to comment upon the extent of their confidence in their advocate. Only two expressed any reservations at all (one of these clients with reservations felt that the advocate was still relatively inexperienced: 'He had not done many cases before; I did not really feel confident').

The overwhelming majority said that they were confident in their advocates: 'He [the advocate] presented the case very well – I had complete confidence at the tribunal.' 'He knew what he was doing all right,' said another. 'Yes, I had complete confidence.' 'I had heard how he had helped other people in the past.' 'He was very kind,' another added.

So, the vast majority of clients believed both that the TAU service offered a different type of service from traditional advice agencies and that this partnership approach was actually an effective way to take up their welfare rights problems.

Amongst the minority who expressed any reservations it is important to note the sense of the partiality of DHSS in general and the tribunal procedure in particular. Several commented, for example, that however effectively TAU had presented their case for them, it would have been a waste of time because the tribunal had been so biased against them: 'In my case, yes [it was a waste of time] – I knew as soon as I went in, because of that man [DHSS officer] who was up against me,' said one. 'I wouldn't go again,' another commented. 'The tribunal does not have time for you.' 'I felt that there was no point – I would not get anything from DHSS,' said a third.

This sense of partiality also emerged when clients were asked if they felt, in the light of their experience, that trained advocates were really necessary at tribunals. DHSS is, after all, supposed to present the case impartially anyway. The majority of those who answered this question believed that trained advocates were essential specifically because of the bias of the DHSS presentation: 'Cases are discussed and decided before tribunals.' 'The tribunal returned a verdict within 30 seconds.' 'If there is no one to represent you, DHSS do not explain everything,' said another. 'DHSS is one-sided.' 'DHSS is completely biased.' 'You've got to have an advocate or they'll walk all over you – push you down if they can,' another commented. 'They refused me my rights on one occasion,' concluded another respondent, 'but they changed their decision after I was represented at a tribunal.' 'DHSS is not impartial, they are out to save money,' was the verdict of yet another client. 'Social security do not represent your case fairly.' Advocates were considered essential to 'counteract this bias'.

Finally, clients were asked if they would use the TAU service again, if they were faced with a similar problem. The vast majority said that they would do so: 'Yes, definitely.' 'Yes, because they have been very helpful.' 'Who else could I go to?' 'I go to them first because they're Jim and John,' said another expressing his personal confidence in his advocates. 'I've got confidence in them.' 'There is no other group like them in the area.' 'Every time you get satisfaction there,' commented another client. 'They did such a good job last time.' Other comments referred to the easy accessibility of TAU volunteers ('I keep their phone number handy') and the fact that the volunteers always explained the issues to their clients. Only one client commented that he might not use the TAU service again because of reservations about TAU itself; this client was disappointed and felt that his advocate had been insufficiently experienced 'to deal with the social security people'.

One client did feel, however, that the bias of DHSS was so overwhelming that it would be pointless to take up any other welfare rights issue in future: 'No disrespect to TAU, but they're flogging a dead horse – you can't beat the system.'

This problem of the bias within 'the system' emerged throughout the client interviews. The general view, however, was more positive. TAU was needed, it was believed, to help people to understand their welfare rights and to press for their entitlements: 'Without TAU the DHSS's word would be law.' 'A lot of people – working-class people – would be put down, would be walked upon.' 'The loss of TAU would be disastrous,' one claimant commented, 'the whole community would suffer.'

Overall, then, the clients' perceptions bore out the views of both the volunteers and the TAU project organisers. The service was valued both in terms of its effectiveness in obtaining welfare rights and for the partnership approach which the local volunteers had developed.

Tribunal chairpersons and members

In contrast, the interviews with tribunal chairpersons and members were somewhat frustrating, because the majority said that they did not know of the TAU service (which severely limited their ability to comment). As it turned out, however, this lack of acquaintance with the work of TAU was typically due to the fact that the chairpersons and members knew the representatives in other capacities rather than of TAU (e.g., as friends or social workers of the clients). 'I had not heard of the service,' said one, for example, 'the representatives never introduced themselves as coming from TAU.' In fact, it emerged that several of the respondents had conducted cases with TAU representatives, but had identified the TAU as simply the friend of the claimant.

Despite these limitations, these interviews did nevertheless produce some confirmation of TAU's assumption that tribunal chairpersons and members can benefit, too, from clients being properly represented. One commented, for example, that claimants could often give information which would help their case, but were unaware of what information they should volunteer. Tribunal members often felt it was impossible to ask the right questions to prompt claimants to give information due to insufficient background knowledge. Representatives were a great help in providing this.

Those with prior knowledge all felt positively about TAU's work in representing clients and helping them to secure their rights: 'They play a role in assisting and educating people to represent themselves and other people at tribunals.' 'They ensure that people know of their rights and have the opportunity to obtain them.' One felt, however, that TAU's intervention was basically individualist – helping people as individuals which had little effect on the operation of the tribunal system more generally.

All those with prior knowledge of TAU felt that overall it was making a positive rather than a negative contribution to the work of the tribunal. 'Any representation is good,' added one of them.

Only a minority of the respondents felt able to offer any comments as to whether or not TAU-represented clients understood the issues and procedures involved in the tribunal. One felt quite simply that they did. Another felt that only a minority of clients overall achieved this, although they were immediately recognisable: 'very few do and you can recognise them almost immediately' for being so uncharacteristic of the normal client. A third felt that at least the TAU-represented clients understood the procedures and were thus more at ease, and less worried by the tribunal procedure.

The respondents were also asked to compare TAU clients with unrepresented clients. The TAU-represented clients 'are more versed . . . knowing what to face,' one felt. 'The more articulate and aware claimants would understand anyway, but all the TAU-represented claimants show greater understanding than could be expected of non-represented claimants,' commented another. 'Probably TAU clients' understanding is a tutored one,' commented a third. 'There is certainly a notable difference (in general) with clients who are represented,' said another.

Overall, then, despite all the limitations on their knowledge of the TAU project, tribunal chairpersons and members were positive, both in their assessment of what they did know about the project and about the representation of appellants more generally.

Building on the TAU experience

The TAU partnership between clients and advocates was justifiably considered as a major achievement. The use of local community volunteers, in this way, represented a novel approach in tribunal access work. As Luba's study, for example, argued, TAU was 'a unique experiment in the field of tribunal assistance services and its evaluation, therefore, had much to contribute to a wider discussion of the "type" and "form" of such agencies at a national level.'[34]

The TAU experience demonstrated that there was, indeed, an untapped pool of potential volunteers in the Welsh mining valleys and that these lay advocates reached their clients and represented them successfully in a way in which professional advocates could rarely achieve. The clients' own understanding was typically enhanced through the process and their active involvement engaged. This factor itself represented a formidable achievement. It did seem clear that (as Bond and Butcher, for example, had suggested) if representation was to support the client rather than merely to reinforce his or her sense of powerlessness, then this representation had to be provided on the *client's own terms*.

The TAU experiment, however, was concerned not merely with the style of information provision and advocacy, but with the development of these resources with the local community, as part of a wider process of organisation building.

Towards the end of the project's funding, the local volunteer group did form a federation, which potentially opened a new phase in welfare rights' organisation in the area. In moving towards this achievement, however, TAU had experienced considerable tensions between providing individual case work and developing collective resources. Their strategy necessitated the provision of both types of support, yet these were also potentially in competition with the project's very limited resources. As the introduction to this chapter has already suggested, tensions between the two approaches as well as their necessary and more creative inter-actions have been experienced far more widely in the provision of information, advice and advocacy.

TAU's success in ultimately combining the two despite these tensions required both time and resources. Had the project been more adequately resourced, more could probably have been achieved in a shorter time period.

More generally, in conclusion, the project work which has been discussed in this chapter would seem to illustrate, too, both some of the relationships and some of the discontinuities between theory and practice. Whilst the projects *were* all engaged in information/advice, training and advocacy work, these activities were not necessarily neatly containable within the original definitions of the middle-ground. The relationship between information and organisation were perceived as relevant, for example, in radical as well as in more technical terms, and these contrasting views did represent considerable and significant differences of emphasis. But, on the other hand, none of the projects was readily categorisable, in respect of each and every specific form of intervention. Individual case work necessarily features within the strategies of projects which emphasised client self-organisation, for example; and similarly the provision of newsletters, and information sheets was not, in itself, ultimately indicative of whether or how these activities related to the projects' overall strategy, whether this was radical, or more closely within the middle-ground of the pluralist spectrum.

5 Employment

With the number of those unemployed in Britain over 3.3 million, and still rising, the significance of the jobs issue scarcely needs underlining in the present context. But when the resource centres were developing their strategies and allocating their priorities in the mid seventies, the objective evidence, in terms of those registered as unemployed, was considerably less stark than now, although the situation was deteriorating rapidly. Unemployment in Britain had been rising since the sixties, but the rate was 3 per cent at the beginning of 1975.[1] From then onwards, however, the total of those unemployed rose steeply with over a million unemployed by the end of 1975, reaching $1\frac{1}{2}$ million in 1976.

One strand in the resource centres' interest in the employment issue, then, can be traced simply in terms of the objective situation – the alarming rise in unemployment and the increasing predominance which the jobs question began to take upon the political agenda. Community workers in general were responding to this situation by showing greater concern for employment issues, for example the Association of Community Workers' Conference in 1977 was centred around the theme of employment.

But it seems clear that the resource centres' developing interest in employment issues did not merely represent a response to changes in the objective situation. The employment question had already been lodged upon the community work agenda from the early seventies, particularly as part of the literature dealing with the political economy of deprived areas. By the end of the seventies, the Political Economy Collective (PEC) representing various CDP projects, had become a major influence in promoting these discussions, (although clearly CDP was neither the only influence nor indeed the only theoretical perspective).

As the CDP report 'Gilding the ghetto' argued, for example, CDP was set up on the assumption that the problems of deprived areas, 'areas of special social need', affected only small groups in marginal areas.[2] Whereas the CDP projects' own analysis led them to emphasise not the *exceptional* or marginal nature of their project areas, but their underlying *similarities* in terms of their relationships to private capital.

Early in the sixties, as 'Gilding the ghetto' argued,[3]

> it became obvious that industry would have to find ways of increasing investment and improving productivity if it was to survive on the basis of private profitability. The process that followed, a process which was in fact facilitated by state intervention to promote industrial rationalisation, had dire consequences particularly for the older urban areas.

As the CDP report, 'The costs of industrial change', had already set out, the restructuring of private capital to maintain profitability in the sixties and seventies involved a dramatic process of shaking out labour with accompanying rises in unemployment and social deprivation in the CDP project areas. 'The story of these places,' 'The costs of industrial change' explained, 'revealed processes at work within the British economy, processes which produce dereliction, redundancies and decline. Where new enterprises did come into these areas, it was typically to take advantage of their cheap sites and vulnerable labour forces, all too often offering low paid work in poor conditions.'[4]

To summarise the argument of 'The costs of industrial change', the decline of each area's industrial structure was seen to have set off 'a chain reaction of economic and social consequences, undermining every aspect of life in the local community'.[5]

For these CDP projects the implications to be drawn from such a conclusion were twofold: firstly, there was no way in which community-work interventions in such areas could attempt to tackle the causes of social deprivation without taking account of the underlying processes of economic decline, and secondly that any effective action must ultimately involve not only local community organisations but the organisations too, of the Labour movement. The case for such conclusions was developed, for example, as it has already been suggested in Chapter 2, in the article by David Corkey and Gary Craig, 'CDP – community work or class politics?' They set out their view of[6]

> why poverty and deprivation are a consequence, not of the deficiencies and habits of the poor themselves, but [are] caused by and maintained of necessity by our present capitalist society, and that what is required is for tenants and residents to join in collective action with those in the Labour Movement . . . active in the class struggle.

As it has been discussed too, in Chapter 2, certain critics have emphasised that CDP, as an example of a radical perspective, was strong on analysis without suggesting the content or even the parameters of a radical *practice* around the issues of jobs and the local economy which involved precisely such alliances between community organisations on the one hand, and organised labour on the other.[7] In practice, however, supporting joint community and trade union action on jobs, the local economy and the related issues of cuts and the loss of jobs and services in the public sector became characteristic of many of the resource centres which were established in the latter half of the seventies, in the wake of the CDP experience.

Concern with the local economy of deprived areas was certainly not, however, confined to those who shared the analysis of, for example, Corkey and Craig. On the contrary, in fact, the jobs issue and the context of industrial reorganisation and decline was identified from the range of competing perspectives – for example, in the Inner Area Studies Report[8], and in the conclusions of Peter Walker, the Conservative minister, who commissioned these studies. In an article in a collection of essays on 'The crisis of the inner city', Walker cited unemployment first in his list of underlying problems, with a positive programme for full employment as top on his list of remedies: 'A positive programme for improving employment opportunities in the Inner City areas' was, Walker concluded, an urgent necessity.[9] The Inner Urban Areas Act, 1977, introducing policies to assist in reviving small-scale industries in declining urban areas, was, although a Labour Party initiative, in practice, a bipartisan policy which survived a change of national government.

In both major political parties in the mid to late seventies, the predominant pluralist/Buskellite assumptions were that, while the restructuring process was an essential and therefore desirable prerequisite for restoring profitability, the costs of restructuring could and should be mitigated, particularly in areas of already high unemployment levels. Although the investment decisions of large, and especially multi-national corporations, were necessarily affected by wider factors, small firms, at least, might be encouraged to fill some part of the widening employment gap in older industrial areas such as the inner cities, without negating the wider strategy of restoring profitability based upon market, rather than social, criteria.

This bipartisan emphasis upon small firms was, of course, criticised, in turn, from the left as representing part of the increasing exploitation of the already vulnerable labour forces in these declining areas. Davis and Green,[10] for example, offer an account of the threat which small firms on the margins of the 'black economy' could pose to local communities and organised labour.

The underlying assumptions about the role of the state in promoting industrial reorganisation were also challenged, not only from outside the major political parties, but also from within them, although the nature of the debates within the Labour Party were perhaps not widely understood outside the party itself until later. 'State intervention in industry',[11] for example, discusses these internal debates within the Labour Party, including the struggles around the direction which the National Enterprise Board should take as a force for preserving jobs through public sector intervention – the Benn view – or as a force for rationalising and thus ultimately destroying jobs, the view that in fact prevailed, the report argued. As the jobs crisis deepened at the end of the seventies, these internal divergences within the major political parties became more widely evident in the sharper climate of political debate. The point to emphasise, then, is that concern for the local economy and employment opportunities in deprived areas covered a broad spectrum of political views and competing theoretical perspectives. While the analysis which 'The costs of industrial change', for example, represented was a crucial influence on the thinking and the subsequent strategies developed by a range of community projects, this was most certainly not the only strand. As the unemployment problem grew more serious in the latter half of the seventies, jobs became an increasingly popular issue for community work intervention and as the range of jobs projects extended, so these differences in perspective and practice and the struggles between and around them became more visible. By the eighties the new right strategy (as exemplified, for example, in the outcome of Heseltine's visit to Liverpool in the summer of 1981, following the Toxteth riots) was to promote jobs through the support of indigenous entrepreneurship; unleashing the barriers to private enterprise. In practice, the solutions to the inner city jobs crisis, formed by certain members of the SDP prominent in this field, were essentially not dissimilar (for example, Peter Hall's emphasis upon the relevance of both small firms and the informal economy in the development of entrepreneurship in the inner city region[12]).

Meanwhile, at local government level, in those authorities where radical forces gained control (notably GLC, Sheffield and West Midlands), there were attempts to operationalise local employment strategies based upon a fundamentally contrasting approach – however problematic in practice. The emphasis was upon the public rather than the private sector, and with an emphasis upon social accountability (for example, via good employer clauses) where public money was invested in job creation/preservation strategies in the private sector, together with a focus upon developing socially useful production and upon the development of alternative (co-operative rather than hierarchical) working relationships planned from the 'bottom up'. As Mike Ward, chairman of the GLC Industry and Employment Committee, argued in a pamphlet drawing explicitly on the experiences of the CDP Interproject reports to develop an alternative local government strategy:[13]

> It is not the purpose of this pamphlet to argue that capitalism can be tamed or transformed by a series of local initiatives, or to adopt an a-theoretical, romantic, 'small is beautiful' approach. To do that would be to deny the class nature of the State; the power of capital cannot be transcended simply by opting out of capitalism, and there is no future in simply building islands of local socialism. There is a need for a national programme of re-industrialisation, and a need for new national institutions to finance that programme. The Labour

Party, the TUC, the IWC and other bodies have begun to develop ideas on the content of such a programme.

But the lesson of the period since 1964 in particular must be that that national programme cannot simply be handed down from above; it must proceed on a basis of active campaigning support. In turn, this means that the elements of the programme need to be developed from below: industrial planning needs to come from the Labour movement and community organisations. That is the importance of the demand for accountability; accountability entails using the position of elected representatives to carry out the priorities determined by these organisations.

The programme for particular industries, for particular communities, for particular regions, must be hammered out in the light of the views and experience of working people in those industries, communities and regions. And the building of local alternatives to the existing economic structure is a vital part of that campaign.

The questions had moved on from whether or not 'jobs' was on the community work agenda, to how and why particular strategies might be justified, how any inherent tensions between them could be contained (or not), and in whose ultimate interests.

But to return to the mid seventies, broadly, jobs projects at that time could be categorised as falling into four types, each of which required community work support, potentially both in terms of background, research and in terms of action:

1 action around planning and policy making;
2 job creation projects;
3 job preservation projects, and (especially subsequently in the seventies) projects to reach the unemployed.

While different theoretical perspectives have tended to lead to different emphases which themselves illustrate the competition between the different perspectives, there has, however, as in information and advocacy work, been no neat correspondence. For example, although local authority planning and policy-making on employment has been a concern of local politicians without any claim to radical credentials, it has also involved trade unionists and community activists (e.g., in Docklands, London); in fact, the report on 'State intervention in industry', produced by the trades councils of Coventry, Liverpool, Newcastle and North Tyneside, specifically calls for a new, more locally and democratically based involvement in policy-making on employment issues (as envisaged subsequently in the local enterprise boards, e.g., in Greater London and West Midlands).

Job creation schemes, too, have been undertaken as part of a range of strategies and perspectives; although there has been some tendency to focus upon the functions of job creation schemes in relation to goals of market intervention (to hold down the relative wages of young people, in particular) and in relation to social control functions, job creation schemes have also been developed from an alternative perspective.

Similarly, schemes to reach the unemployed have ranged from the provision of welfare rights information, including the suggestion of military service for unemployed youth as an alternative to the dole queue, through the more characteristically pluralist approach of providing information and welfare, through again to the more overtly radical approach of centres such as the Newcastle-upon-Tyne Trades Council's centre for the unemployed.[14] The aim of this pioneering centre has been not only to provide facilities and information, backed up by research, but to support the self-organisation of the unemployed, as part of a vigorous campaign against unemployment within the community and the trade union movement.

As the centre itself explained, 'we shall continue to tackle the "scrounger myth" and we shall continue to build in the closest alliances with Trade Unionists on the one hand and the unemployed workers union on the other – a positive and hopeful alternative to the scourge of mass unemployment.'[15] Society must, the centre argues, be made fully aware both of the great suffering brought about by unemployment and of other positive alternatives, including alternative worker's plans (such as those of the Lucas Aerospace Shop Stewards Combine Committee and the Vickers Shop Stewards Combine Committee) for new socially useful products.

Since the Newcastle centre was established, a range of centres have been set up, in other areas, with varying emphasis upon welfare and/or collective self-organisation, a development which gathered momentum with the political prominence of the issue of organising the unemployed, around the People's March for Jobs in 1981. The TUC, too, has given recognition to the key significance of organising the unemployed, and providing local centres where advice is also available.[16] And once again, as it has already been suggested in Chapter 4, self-organisation strategies have not implied any sectarian rejection of the provision of practical advice and support on rights and benefits as well; rather the issue has been that of relative balance between these different aspects, in relation to each of the centres' longer-term strategies.

One further aspect of community-based organisation around jobs, in relation to the organisation of the unemployed, has been the issue of women's employment and unemployment. Women's unemployment, as measured by registered unemployment figures, has risen far more dramatically even than men's (between 1971 and 1980 women's unemployment rose by 414 per cent compared with an increase of 84 per cent for men). Yet even these figures understate the full extent of women's unemployment since women's registration is neither comprehensive (registration being related to entitlement or lack of entitlement to welfare), nor consistent over time. Following the phasing out of married women's national insurance contributions in 1977, more women would have been expected to register as unemployed in order to claim benefit in their own right, a situation which could be reversed once again by changes in registration procedures. (Estimates of the proportion of unregistered to registered unemployed women were still the same, $2\frac{1}{2}$ to 1, in 1981.)

The point to emphasise here is simply that women's situation at work and out of work cannot even be measured accurately, let alone analysed without reference to women's status and specifically women's dependent status within the family. Typically, the expectation that young women will subsequently leave the labour market for a period to bear and rear their children is related to their concentration in jobs which are defined as non-career jobs; jobs for which formally validated skills and training are often not required. The vulnerability of their labour market position becomes even more evident if and when women return to work, particularly as secondary-status, part-time workers, fitting in their jobs around their domestic commitments. Formally, equality of opportunity is guaranteed by the Equal Pay and Sex Discrimination Act, and those individual women who can fit into the requirements of uninterrupted full-time careers can and do combat ideological prejudices to compete with men. But the underlying structure of job segregation has persisted. As the Department of Employment's 1979 survey illustrated, women as a whole remain concentrated in lower-paid and less-organised jobs, with little or no formal skill recognition especially in the service sector, and a limited number of manufacturing industries.

Women's potential vulnerability at work is compounded, too, by the tendency for women with domestic commitments to work part-time (two out of five women work part-time, i.e., less than 30 hours a week). Part-time work has, in fact, been discussed in terms of the ideal-type of the reserve army of labour, or that section which can most readily be drawn into the labour force and then disposed of again, sent back to the home in response to the fluctuating requirements of capital.[17] Unemployed married women have not even needed to be counted as unemployed, once they have exhausted their national insurance benefits and reverted to economic dependence upon their husbands within the family. Conversely, however, the reserve army thesis is not only about greater disposability, but about drawing on cheap and flexible forms of labour, too, as part of the restructuring process, the relative growth of part-time work, for example in the retail industry.

Given the lack of effective trade union organisation and the particular vulnerability of so many women in this situation, moving in and out of relatively casual jobs, traditional forms of workplace organisation are specifically and self-evidently in need of supplementation. Building the links between community and work-based organisations, then, has been predominantly and most specifically an issue in relation to women's employment.

One of the better-known recent examples of radical action illustrating these attempts to link local trade union structures and community organisations was the strike involving Asian women and men at the Grunwick factory in North West London.[18]

There are, of course, a range of less dramatic examples, covering a variety of perspectives and strategic attempts to involve women's organisations, using local resources, to support the development of trade union organisation (for example, in the retail trade in expanding 'shopping cities'), together with efforts to develop joint positive action strategies in relation to the recipients as well as to the providers of public services.

Women's employment projects have also been concerned both with the provision of research and information support and with the provision of practical support, including training, child-care and job-sharing facilities to enable women to combat job segregation. Local projects have also been involved directly with job creation, and with the development of women's co-operatives.[19] This involvement in co-operative development has been specifically justified in relation to women's employment, as a means of breaking down the isolation of women in particularly fragmented and casual employment/unemployment situations, night cleaners and homeworkers, for instance. The Kennington Office Cleaners' Co-op (described in the London Women's Employment Projects' chapter of *Women in Collective Action*[20]) provides such an example, for women who were without alternative forms of employment. Despite initial support from the relevant trade union, however, the women were apparently uninterested in becoming union members, and, however understandable such a perspective was from their viewpoint, it was a perspective which involved a certain potential for arousing traditional trade union suspicions of co-operative developments.

The point of illustrating certain potential tensions, however, is *not* to suggest that the development of women's co-operatives can necessarily be defined *only* in terms of any one particular perspective and strategy (or as one which is necessarily implicitly hostile to the organised labour movement at all). Certain parallels to these potential tensions can be traced more generally, too, in the subsequent case histories, dealing with men's as well as women's employment.

The area resource centres and employment

Coming back, however, to the resource centres' experiences, those area resource centres which included employment work effectively covered the range of projects and strategies, typically focusing upon both the issues of job creation and job preservation. SWAPAC also covered other types of intervention at various phases of its development, in so far as the centre had included a general commitment to feedback for policy formation, and the TAU project had included the unemployed in their programme to support the self-organisation of claimants.

In general, however, there was *initially* more emphasis upon job creation projects, and *subsequently* more interest in supporting job preservation struggles as part of joint trade union and community action, although both CWS and SWAPAC retained, to some extent, either direct or indirect support for job creation schemes, such as co-operatives, in their latter phases. The examples from SWAPAC and from Govan, which are described in the second half of this chapter, illustrate some of the reasons for these shifts of emphasis and some of the potential tensions inherent in focusing upon both job creation and job preservation strategies, at that period, while retaining the active involvement of both community and trade union activists.

It is, perhaps, worth emphasising at this point, that, as already suggested, the purpose of this discussion of some of the possible contradictions involved in job creation, and particularly in co-operative job creation ventures, is not to imply that such strategies could or should simply be ruled out of court, at least from the perspective of a radical strategy. In fact co-operative development, as a means of developing alternative working relations, has appeared within the employment programme of radical local authorities, for example, and was still firmly on the agenda at the beginning of the eighties. The point, then, is not to dismiss such developments, out of hand, so much as to re-emphasise not only their most obvious limitations (in terms of the numbers of jobs which can be created and in terms of the limits placed upon their operations, ultimately, through the operations of market criteria of profitability), but also the necessity for counteracting their operational difficulties, including at times potentially negative and divisive impact upon local community groups, and in particular between them and the trade union movement.

The case study of employment work in Govan which follows also illustrates some of the tensions inherent in a strategy which attempted to combine not only job preservation and job creation, but co-operative employment involving both workers' self-management *and* success in terms of market criteria. Finally, co-operative developments in this case study represented, too, a meeting point for the exponents of small business type solutions through to the exponents of libertarian socialist strategies.

Through understanding some of the underlying difficulties which the resource centre faced in attempting to combine these goals and to accommodate the varying theoretical perspectives in the causation, and thus the possible range of policy alternatives appropriate to grappling with the growing unemployment problem, it may become easier to understand both what could have been done to minimise these difficulties and the reasons for the different strategic choices which were eventually adopted.

The employment work in GARC's strategy

Employment, and more specifically unemployment, was identified as a key problem in Govan, virtually from the outset. The first annual report to the commission, produced in October 1977, when GARC had been functioning for only three months, already identified as an objective the organisation of a study group on the local employment situation. In fact, industrial change and the de-industrialisation process's social effects formed a key element in that report's introduction, identifying the problems of the area:[21]

> Nothing has come to fill the employment gap left by the
> disappearance of ship-building and its related industries. That,
> coupled with insensitive redevelopment policies were associated
> with the 'now scarcely visible' spirit of the 'once thriving
> community'.

'Between 1964 and 1974,' the report continued, 'the number of jobs available in Glasgow declined by 102,600, of which 86,888 were for males and 15,712 for females,' with the result that 'male unemployment in the area [Glasgow] was running as high as 14%....'[22] 'Industrial decline in ship-building and engineering has left Glasgow as the most deprived city in the UK ...'.[23] The report also referred to, and drew parallels with, the findings of the Coventry and West Glamorgan CDPs, i.e., that the problems of these areas derived from structural changes in their local economies and the consequent social effects of industrial decline. Employment/unemployment in the context of industrial change was clearly seen by the project staff, at least, as the lynchpin of Govan's problems. This view was evidently shared by the management committee. The second annual report (November 1978) commented: 'Almost from the inception, the Management Committee realised the important role that the Centre could play in the field of employment.'[24] This was confirmed at the management committee in March 1978 which gave top priority to employment work and allocated one worker's time to it. Since one of the three staff was an administrator, this represented the effective allocation of 50 per cent of the community work support to employment. From personal discussions with the staff it would seem that the opportunity costs of such a decision had been weighed up and considered to have been fully justified by the objective gravity of the employment situation and its relevance in terms of the staff's analysis of the underlying causes of social deprivation.

It was decided to invite a balanced group of participants, representing community and trade union activists and concerned professionals, to set up an employment study group (ESG) in November 1977. The intention was to create a forum to reflect upon the issues and upon possible solutions to them for a period of some six months and then to produce a report. After this six months' period, it was anticipated that GARC would be in a far better position to develop a coherent strategy for its employment work: 'The Employment Study Group would provide a debating arena – the policy outcomes were to emerge – they were not clearly established at that point in time.' It was to 'create the environment for debate and action on unemployment by community groups in Govan.'[25]

The original brief of the ESG was to focus upon the most acute employment problems of the young (e.g., school-leavers) and the over-forties. Attempts to concentrate only upon the former so that the project could focus upon job creation project-type pro-grammes were, however, resisted, in an attempt to keep the broader options open. There was to be space for a broad strategy to emerge, not simply a job creation strategy for the young or older unemployed.

The original members of the ESG, eight of whom attended the founding meeting, included both those with professional interests (e.g., training, community work and management) and com-munity activists, including several trade union activists.

Subsequent decision points for the employment work

There seem to have been two major options in relation to the development of the employment work – should it focus upon the causes of the de-industrialisation process in Govan and upon lobbying or otherwise organising within the locality and within the Labour movement to press for policy changes to a macro-level as well as a local level, or should the project concentrate upon self-help initiatives in terms of employment creation locally?

Two of the staff who were most closely involved at the earliest stages felt quite clearly that both policy options were essential and mutually interdependent:[26]

> One strand was job creation, the other strand was analysing the employment situation, with a view to producing a report and possibly to further action such as lobbying. It was a two-pronged approach, but the second strand did not materialise.

In practice there were tensions. Subsequent interviews with key participants revealed some of the implications of this process of decision-making. There would seem to have been two principal reasons for the direction which the ESG eventually took. The first was GARC's appointment of a specialist adviser with expertise in co-operative development. Having a specialist within the group could be related to the general shift of focus towards his area of expertise, whether as cause or effect, or most probably as some combination of both. In any event, looking back at the end of that first full operational year (1978), GARC commented that 'the group [ESG] very quickly came to the conclusion that the unemployment situation was very serious and that it was essential for the community to take an active part in promoting and creating employment.'[27] A further factor in this decision-making process was the group's own impatience with discussion and their very understandable desire to achieve something concrete.

At this point, events seem to have taken on a dynamic of their own. The group's enthusiasm for the suggestion for setting up a venture of their own (a co-operative wholefood store called the Grain Store) led to a feasibility study being produced, and premises being found (all by the end of May 1978). GARC offered £500 backing and the official opening took place in August 1978.

This Grain Store employed two member-workers who concentrated upon selling grain, fruit and vegetables; this was felt to constitute a valuable and 'socially useful' service to the local community, as well as being a modest source of employment gain for the two member-workers concerned.

Problems, however, seem to have emerged right from the start. Without elaborating on these problems in any detail, they may be summarised as focusing upon inadequate starting capital, insufficient management expertise and experience, and unclear lines of responsibility between the member-workers and the rest of the ESG. There were some unlucky accidents, too, such as the purchase of a car (for transporting goods) which 'died'. By October, the finances were described as being 'in a mess'. Over this period, the workers agreed to cut their salaries by half (to only £25 per week) and to sell the car. One of the GARC staff was brought in to help sort out the books.

Meanwhile, the two Grain Store member-workers left, apparently in some disillusion. The Grain Store itself continued trading, but with constant financial difficulty. Even by 1980, it was apparently not fully viable commercially, and still needed support via GARC. The Grain Store was also taking up increasing amounts of staff time both from the GARC community worker and from the book-keeper. As the 1978 annual report commented, more generally, of the employment work, 'it has to be recognised that these projects consume quite a large proportion of the total resources of the Centre; this is due to the complex and pioneering nature of these activities such as the development of the skill of unemployed people in being able to manage enterprises'[28] – a prophetic underestimation of the sheer practical difficulties of launching a profitable business on such a basis.

GARC, then, was providing at least one of their two community workers'/organisers' worktime in return for supporting a project over which it had no direct control, which was not yet showing any sign of becoming financially viable and which had failed, so far, to provide reasonably paid jobs even to the two initial workers. Worse still, the co-operative venture was actually leading to dissension locally.

Overall, two processes seemed to have been occurring. On the one hand, some of the early participants in the ESG evidently withdrew, either because of their disillusionment with the Grain

Store experience, or more generally, perhaps, because they had been more interested in the other main strand of the employment work – the report on de-industrialisation and job preservation struggles. On the other hand, there was increasing emphasis on expertise and particularly on business expertise and management skills. Clearly no co-operative or community venture can afford to run at a loss, and if the venture yields no profits, the prospects for further community enterprise developments are by definition non-starters. But the emphasis upon professional management skills was a further potential source of tension with, and distance from, local working-class activists.

This shift in emphasis was symbolised by the establishment of a formal company, called Govan Enterprises, in the summer of 1979 when the ESG reconstituted itself as a community company. As the 1979 annual report commented, 'the formation of the multi-purpose company marks a new move away from the ESG policy of "studying" the situation or passively waiting for people to come forward with ideas and helping them form into co-operatives to a much more positive "*entrepreneurial*" policy of starting enterprises and finding the necessary resources in terms of manpower, finance etc., to make these successful.'[29]

Projects then being discussed included an urban gardening project, a TV/electrical shop, a print workshop, a home producers' indoor market, and a recycling outlet. A set of video tapes which were made over that year also included information on how to set up a business, as part of the move to educate local people to be more expert in entrepreneurial skills.

In parallel, a 'Workspace' project (to provide premises for small firms) which had originally been explored in the summer of 1978 was similarly launched to promote small business in the area (although once again, within the overall context of community enterprise, i.e., ploughing back the profits to the local community). A feasibility study was produced in 1979, which demonstrated the demand for workshops (i.e., small factory units for small businesses). On that basis, the Workspace group went ahead with proposals for the acquisition of alternative premises. Once again, according to one of the key informants, by definition, the requirements of developing the Workspace project entailed some considerable expertise (including coping with architects' briefs). In some senses, by definition, success in terms of market criteria was becoming more evidently less and less compatible with the active participation of non-expert, rank-and-file community and trade union activists.

The point to emphasise is simply that not everyone in the Govan working-class community could reasonably be expected to participate fully in such professional/managerial activities. This, then, raises the question of how far this issue was understood in GARC when the original decisions about the employment work, and particularly the co-operative and community enterprises elements in the employment strategy, were first taken. It would, in fact, seem that they were not. It was apparently hoped, simply, that the consultant would provide the technical support, whereas, in practice, the technical and professional requirements seem to have far exceeded the original estimates. The input from GARC staff was evidently also vastly underestimated. Co-ops and small businesses, then, absorbed increasing amounts of staff time (and even that was insufficient as managerial/technical input) in return for a decreasing level of active community involvement.

In retrospect, the increasing emphasis on professionalism/managerial and technical skills may have been inevitable, but this was evidently not fully considered in the spring of 1978 when the key decisions were taken. Nor was the ensuing departure of some of the original local community activist members apparently envisaged, although, once again, perhaps with the wisdom of hindsight, it is possible to discern some of the underlying conflicts of interest between the proponents of socially useful production in co-ops and small businesses on the one hand, and local trade union activists struggling to preserve traditional manufacturing jobs, on the other.

Apart from any reservations which they may or may not have held about job creation projects (on the grounds that they involved as much if not more managerial and professional criteria as opportunities for alternative working relationships based on workers' self-management), the argument of sheer numbers must have been pressing. Literally thousands of traditional jobs were disappearing, while this handful of precarious posts was being so painfully created.

The employment survey

As part of the evaluation process, twenty-three of the twenty-five members of the ESG and the off-shoot Workspace and Govan Enterprises projects who still lived in the area were interviewed; the other two were unavailable for interview at that time. Their replies and comments illustrated both the idealism and commitment of those involved in the attempts to develop co-operative and socially useful production and some of the inherent tensions which have already been outlined above.

At this point, it should also be made clear that these interviews contained certain in-built biases, especially in that the 'professionals' (e.g., the community workers) tended to comment at greater length than the working-class activists, even about aspects of the work with which they had not been directly involved. Since the 'professionals' and managers made up a third or so of the group this affected the replies, although it is, of course, also possible that they affected the ESG group, more generally, and made disproportionate contributions in practice, too.

The participants were asked about the concrete achievements of the ESG. The most important outcomes to be mentioned were not surprisingly Govan Workspace and Govan Enterprises. But a minority felt that nothing very useful had been acheived. The most negative replies all came from the manual workers and the one clerical member, whereas the positive replies came disproportionately from the professional and managerial members. Two of the three who expressed the most negative views of all did subsequently drop out of the employment work, and expressed a range of other negative views in their comments more generally. There had, then, been crucial differences of view within the group.

The decision to set up the Grain Store had, for example, evidently been controversial. Several felt that this had been seized upon as part of the general desire to 'do something concrete' before the implications or possible alternatives had been properly considered. The most critical respondent felt that the decision to set up the Grain Store had been the work of the professionals: 'We [the older trade unionists] were just a bunch of dodos; they did everything and took all the decisions.' But, once the decision to set up the Grain Store had been taken, the pressures of market forces became inevitably increasingly pressing. Finance and management expertise were both in short supply. As one critic commented on the venture, 'it didn't make money,' and as a result 'paid advisers had to be brought in,' thereby shifting the balance of the project still further, this respondent felt, from the local community towards outside professional experts.

Govan Enterprises, itself, emerged as fraught with similar tensions, the aspirations for demonstrating the potential of alternative (co-operative) working relationships on the one hand, set against the pressures for professionalism, if the venture were to be commercially viable, on the other. This need to emphasise professionalism and managerial skills, if any of these ventures were to be successful, emerged once again in the subsequent discussions.

From the more open-ended questions in the survey, it emerged that the community workers and the other professionals were ultimately more optimistic about the prospects for small businesses, including co-ops based on alternative working relations. Those who had been more directly involved in industry, whether as managers or employees, tended, in contrast, to emphasise macro-economic solutions to Govan's employment problems, from the need to modernise industry to demands for reflating the national economy, and investing in public sector employment, locally as well as nationally.

While the majority of those involved had considerable praise for the dedicated work of the GARC staff in supporting the employment work, several also expressed doubts about whether the results could really justify such inputs of time and energy: 'There is a lot of time and money invested for very, very small returns,' said one, for example. 'I think that the concept of Workspace is a good one, but I doubt if GARC can afford the time and staff input,' commented another.

To summarise, then, the debate focused around whether sufficient dents could be made into market forces in Govan via socially useful schemes and/or the promotion of financially viable small businesses, and whether the process of attempting to do so was too costly either in terms of the necessary community work input, or in terms of the inherent potential conflicts with other goals including the active involvement of local trade union and community activists.

SWAPAC – some comparisons and contrasts

As the second example of a resource centre concerned with employment work demonstrated, SWAPAC faced very similar issues in developing and then in restructuring its own strategies.

Employment was identified as a key area of concern in the 1976 progress report (part II) – an overwhelming problem again in terms of the objective evidence. Unemployment figures (then 82,500 in Wales, or 8 per cent compared with 6.1 per cent in Great Britain as a whole) were cited as 'the single most important index . . . in a series of indices of deprivation'.[30] Even this average figure of 8 per cent concealed higher local concentrations; for example, some unemployment rates were 40-50 per cent higher in the inner city areas. In some of the valleys, rates were as high as 13 per cent (e.g., Bargoed), which meant, as the report pointed out, that 'more than 3,000 people were out of work in an employable population of less than 25,000.'[31] 'In terms of the economy,' the report continued, 'poverty has been aggravated and deepened by the reliance upon declining primary industries . . . leading to high concentrations of unemployment in some areas and extremely high concentrations grouped in scattered pockets in relatively isolated settlements.'[32]

SWAPAC started from the assumption that 'given the scale of deprivation and its structural causes', there was no way in which self-help initiatives could be seen as a 'panacea'.[33] Self-help could not be effective without greater resources, financial and otherwise, being made available. Nevertheless, SWAPAC, at this period, emphasised the value of self-help as representing a qualitatively different approach offering the means for developing new forms of social relationships:[34]

> The need is for social relationships which are co-operative
> rather than dominating, democratic rather than hierachical,
> and caring rather than exploitative. It is in the role that self-
> help groups can play in the developing of these new forms of
> social relationships that their greatest potential contribution in
> combating poverty is to be found.

Such an approach led to a more specific initial employment strategy than that sponsored in Govan. The focus was quite explicitly[35]

Information and Advice to Self-Help Groups . . . to help in the promotion and development and management of local employment initiatives which are commercially viable, with particular emphasis upon the potential of the Job Creation Programme (JCP) as a 'pump-priming operation' to launch ventures which could then become commercially viable co-operatives enterprises.

Some of the difficulties were also identified. It was recognised, for example, that the most disadvantaged and especially the long-term unemployed might be least likely to be able to take up the possibilities offered by JCP schemes for instance, let alone for longer-term, commercially viable co-operative employment.

Equally, it was recognised that the institutions of labour (i.e., the trade unions) as well as those of capital espoused ideologies which 'did not in general favour initiatives of small independent co operative ventures by working people'.[36] While contact with trade unions had been attempted and was still considered desirable SWAPAC recognised the differences of interest and the material basis for the trade unions' suspicion.

The need for co-operative ventures to be commercially viable was also given prominence (another element in the potential conflict between the ideology of socially useful co-operative production on the one hand and the requirements of the private market on the other). It was recognised, too, that, even if labour-intensive projects were given priority, the number of jobs likely to be created would be small. Nevertheless, even if yielding small numbers of jobs, these ventures would, it was believed, make considerable demands on SWAPAC's time, where intensive support was required and even where less extensive help was to be provided.

One particular member of staff was identified as having the necessary skills, and funds were ear-marked for consultancy. Addtionally, a worker who had been taken on under the University of Aston Inter-Disciplinary Higher Degrees Scheme was undertaking relevant project work which would, it was hoped, be supportive. The WEA had also been contacted for support with a co-operative employment educational programme.

This, then, was the initial SWAPAC employment strategy, and the resources committed to implementing it. Between 1976 and

1977, however, there were major shifts of focus within SWAPAC as part of their appraisal of the initial experience.

The broader employment situation had in any case altered, having deteriorated alarmingly in terms of both the total jobs available and the consequent unemployment levels, and in terms of wages and take-home pay (particularly as a result of the policy of pay restraints). Public sector jobs were hit especially hard, both as a result of the 'voluntary' pay code which was far more readily enforceable in the public sector, and as a result of public expenditure cuts, which resulted in frozen posts. 'It is,' the report continued,' 'becoming increasingly apparent that the present high rate of unemployment is not the ebb of an economic cycle but is part of a continuing chronic decline in employment in the industrial sector. . . . Against this ominous macro-economic background,' the report concluded, 'the contribution of community action in the fight against poverty has to be seen as operating at a relatively low level.'[37]

In terms of the employment work, this perspective provided part of the explanation for the shift in emphasis away from job creation and self-help co-operative developments. Reflecting on their work for the previous year in supporting JCP initiatives and co-operative development, SWAPAC concluded that there were inherent tensions and contradictions. While re-affirming the value of assisting local groups to secure and manage resources themselves, SWAPAC was concerned that:

> employment under such programmes is generally little more than a short-term relief, which seems designed to bear out the conception of unemployment as a cyclical inevitability. . . . The programmes as a whole do not confront, but divert attention from the problem of chronic structural unemployment. If SWAPAC is to move forward from this contradiction, while preserving its commitment to supporting self-help groups, its future work in the employment field must have greater regard to the need to draw in trade union activists to provide a wider, less introspective dimension to any local employment initiatives and generally to encourage the adoption of a wider perspective on employment conditions in South Wales.

A key element in SWAPAC's strategy became precisely this focus upon analysing the dynamics of the de-industrialisation process and its social effects in South Wales, to produce relevant information and to share their understanding of the problems with the local Labour movement.

In terms of the initial focus of SWAPAC's employment work (on job creation and co-ops), there were additional reasons for the shift of emphasis. The first year's experience was in some senses highly productive (for example, SWAPAC supported the establishment of a knitwear co-operative – formed by redundant textile workers – by providing advice and consultancy money to prepare a feasibility study and to secure JCP financing).

Nevertheless, SWAPAC concluded:[38]

> it has become apparent that the assistance which SWAPAC has to offer in this field is too limited and generalist . . . embryo co-ops need specialist technical advice on finance, production, distribution, marketing and so on. If SWAPAC is to assist co-ops in the future (and it is unlikely that this will be a priority in view of the amount of effort needed to assist a relatively small number of people and in view of the declared preference for working with organised labour), then such help should be directed to encouraging existing co-ops to federate and then themselves establish a specialist agency, directly accountable to them, which will provide the necessary technical support services.

To summarise, a generalist community intervention agency, such as SWAPAC, considered itself to be unsuitable for the most effective provision of such support services, even if co-operative development had remained one of their key priorities. The fact that it did not remain so related to a more general process of prioritising SWAPAC's working strategy. As a result, there was a greater emphasis upon the necessity to assist community groups and organised labour in widening their perspectives and linking their struggles rather than focusing upon potentially introspective self-help projects which resulted in people 'merely administering their own poverty in the illusion that they are taking active measure to arrive at its elimination.'[39]

As SWAPAC had already arrived at the conclusion that its resources were too 'limited and generalist' in nature, other sources of support were developed for co-operative ventures, on the basis of the notion that such ventures needed to establish 'their own intermediary body, to provide and facilitate the exchange of socio-technical support services'.[40]

This was the reason for the establishment of the Welsh Community Enterprise (WCE) agency, which was set up to provide just such services, on the initiative of the ventures themselves over this period, and directly accountable to them. This establishment of WCE represented a significant development both for the co-operative ventures themselves, and for SWAPAC's employment strategy more generally. The ventures' demands for technical and other assistance were being met through their own co-operative and self-sufficient activities, rather than through increasing demands upon SWAPAC staff's time and energies.

For SWAPAC, the establishment of WCE demonstrated the viability of creating self-sustaining initiatives, the model which had, after all, been adopted in their first report. Additionally, of course, hiving off the co-operative development work freed the SWAPAC team to develop the other strands of their employment strategy, in line with the policy change worked through in the previous year. One key element of this developing and more overtly radical strategy was the promotion of links 'between community groups and organised labour' which had been considered so problematic, in relation to the co-operative development work at that period. Some of the first examples of this process of building the links were provided by a series of conferences and papers, on hospital closures and NHS cuts for example, and the research into the organisation and management of direct labour organisation of five housing authorities in South Wales and the consequent backlog of improvement programmes for properties owned by those authorities. 'It is anticipated,' the report concluded, 'that underspending in Central Government allocations could be avoided by the more effective management of resources and through employing unemployed construction workers and youngsters engaged upon temporary employment schemes' (i.e., benefiting both the producers and the recipients of housing services).[41]

A further development of SWAPAC's employment work, at this time, was an emphasis upon the provision of research:[42]

SWAPAC strongly believe that well-researched information provides the best possible foundation for strengthening struggles against unemployment. It will be equally important to begin to outline alternative approaches that might be usefully pursued, for we do not accept that unemployment is inevitable.

The first examples of such research included joint sponsoring of a report with Rhondda trades union council to investigate and report on employment in the Rhondda Valley. At the same time, a second report was being planned with another trades union council, where a large-scale redundancy had recently occurred, to investigate the social and economic consequences of closure.

To summarise, by 1978, SWAPAC had moved in the reverse direction to that being adopted in Govan, over the same period. From an initial focus upon self-help and co-operative development, SWAPAC had succeeded in establishing these as self-sustaining ventures and thereby freed staff time and energy to pursue alternative strategies. These focused upon forging links between community groups and the Labour movement and providing background information and research relevant particularly to job preservation struggles and the broader movement to resist the combined effects of the de-industrialisation process and the public expenditure cuts.

It was believed that until the co-operative, self-help ventures had been assisted in becoming self-sufficient for technical and other support, these alternative strategies could not have been pursued. There would neither have been the resources (including staff time) nor, it was argued, the necessary support, given the potential conflicts of interest inherent in job creation involving small businesses and commercial viability on the one hand and job preservation and the priorities of the Labour movement on the other.

Having developed the rationale for SWAPAC's shift away from job creation towards job preservation strategies and for their increasing focus upon building alliances with the Labour movement, it should be added that the trade union movement's attitude towards job creation and co-operative developments was not a once-and-for-all fixed entity, either. In fact, as the employment situation deteriorated at an increasingly rapid rate over 1980, there was some evidence (particularly in Wales) of greater trade union interest in any possible solution, including co-ops (for example, the Welsh TUC organised a visit to the Mondragon co-op in Spain, early in 1981).

Part of the explanation for such an interest may also be found in the increasing difficulty in sustaining job preservation struggles in the harsher climate of the deepening world recession and the more rapid pace of industrial restructuring favoured by the Thatcher government, with its monetarist economic strategy. This political climate was particularly relevant in South Wales with its dependence upon public sector industries. Maintaining the impetus behind job preservation strategies, when they had so little apparent chance of success, clearly became increasingly problematic for the Labour movement and for those working-class communities which had actively supported resistance to bearing the costs for industrial re-organisation – although there have, of course, been continued struggles, for example amongst the South Wales miners in February 1981.

In these circumstances, campaigns for jobs have, in contrast, become more explicitly concerned to set out alternative scenarios (as in the alternative economic strategy debates) in terms of macro-economic and political strategies at national and international as well as at local level, and in terms of alternative plans for production, based upon meeting social needs through the public sector as well as for demonstrating the viability of alternative working relationships through co-operative development (some of the goals as well as dilemmas inherent in progressive local authority job strategies within the context of the market economy). They have also had to become more explicitly concerned to link the organisations and demands of the Labour movement not only directly with the political process but also with the organisations and demands of those who have never been or may never again be part of organised labour, through such projects as the unemployed workers' centres.

6 Housing and planning

Housing and planning, as issues, in some senses require least introduction in terms of their relevance to community work and community action in the seventies. In the early seventies, as *Community Action* magazine set out in its 50th issue (September/ October 1980), the major emphasis in community action was, after all, on housing and planning.

The early seventies were, of course, a period of major urban redevelopment at a period of booming profits and property development, involving private capital and local political interventions, both indirectly through the planning process, and more directly via development consortia. Some 70,000 dwellings were being cleared per annum in the 1960s – as compared with half that number in the mid 1950s. The nature and implications of this increase in the scale of these interventions has been discussed by a range of authors.[1] One aspect of community action's history at this period can be traced directly back, then, in terms of local responses to these interventions.

For the processes of redevelopment raised a series of questions, as urban populations and, in particular, inner city populations, found their homes and ways of life threatened by planning proposals, for the major redevelopment of whole city centres, as in Manchester or Glasgow, for instance.[2]

Even where there were less drastic schemes, property development produced significant ripple effects on land values, house prices and rents; the 'gentrification' process in areas such as Inner London, for example, created it own community action responses from the beleaguered local communities.[3]

These 'urban social movements' of tenants and residents which emerged on the local political scene as a result were documented and theoretically located initially by the French structuralists,[4] then brought into the British literature in the mid seventies and subjected to critical evaluation[5] as part of the move away from structuralist approaches, as discussed in Chapter 2. The forms of community action which these authors were analysing were not, of course, merely reactive, however, nor were they confined to direct responses to the increasingly intrusive intervention of private capital and the state, at the local level. Local demands for greater participation in planning, and indeed for greater democratic accountability in services more generally, were also part of the broader context of the late 1960s and early 1970s – the period immediately following the student explosions of 1968 – and, in the British context, of an upsurge of activity in the Labour movement, as the first two chapters have already suggested.

In parallel with this more assertive national political mood, local working-class people were expressing demands for a better quality of service (particularly in terms of council house maintenance and repairs) and at a reasonable price.[6]

The early part of the seventies was, as it has been suggested, a period when there were official moves to extend public participation schemes in local government, in planning (Skeffington Report 1969) and in tenant management schemes, for example. The growth of community work itself was, in part at least, a response to such trends.[7]

As it turned out subsequently, the focus of community work and community action clearly shifted over the course of the seventies, particularly after the property boom burst in 1974, and there was less intense concentration upon housing and planning. Meanwhile, other issues, particularly public expenditure cuts, employment, racism, health, education, and women's issues, came to be more clearly lodged upon the community work agenda. The contents of Community Action magazine itself illustrated this broadening of issues over time. Nevertheless, housing and planning do seem to have retained some form of core status in relation to the priorities of community activists and community workers.

Mirroring this, the area resource centres were all concerned to support community work and community action around housing and planning as major aspects of their work. The centres' actual involvement covered a broad range of activities and developing strategies, with differences both between and within centres. CWS, for example, was concerned to support community groups in making inputs on national and regional policy (although CWS was also involved in very local housing work too). The SWAPAC example, on the other hand, illustrates tenants' organisations building a federation at this latter, local end of the operational/organisational spectrum.

In fact, as it has already been argued in relation both to information provision and advocacy, and to employment, it was an essential part of the resource centres' strategy to operate at both these levels, precisely because the more local operations had such a specific input to make to the wider policy discussions. Without the validation of these community-based experiences, the policy inputs would, it was argued, have been merely another set of specialists' views, however radical (or otherwise) these might, in themselves, be. The relevance of the policy inputs which the resource centres supported were very different, however, for they were typically the result of a series of community-based experiences, rather than technical solutions advocated by some other set of experts from outside the situation, however sympathetic to the problems and interests of that community. Yet, without the wider policy framework, these local initiatives would remain fragmented and potentially in competition with each other for scarce resources.

The first example of the CWS support for the Campaign for Family Housing/Homes in Central London illustrates the process of policy inputs being made on housing and planning issues, both at the political level and at a major public inquiry, based upon the collective experience of local community and trade union organisations. This was precisely the type of 'bottom-up' policy-making which was advocated, for example, in relation to employment issues in the conclusion to the trades councils' paper 'State intervention in industry' (discussed in Chapter 5). The more local organisational work upon which these policy inputs were based is discussed in relation to the second example for South Wales, the development of the South Wales Association of Tenants. In each case, the campaign is described in the members' own terms. In the latter case, in fact, when the tenants discussed the personal as well as the political implications of their collective experiences, the role of the evaluator was virtually reduced to that of an editor.

The CWS support for the Campaign for Family Housing/ Campaign for Homes in Central London

CWS offered support to the Campaign for Family Housing (which subsequently became the Campaign for Homes in Central London) from its inception in 1977 through to the conclusion of the evaluation period (1980) and beyond. The campaign itself was an autonomous federal grouping of community organisations across Inner London, which formed itself originally without any initiative from CWS. From then onwards, CWS offered a range of background support services, including the provision of secretarial and organisational services, the use of a meeting room and eventually considerable time inputs from one of the CWS staff. This staff-time involved helping particularly with the provision of background research and information for the campaign's participation in a major public inquiry and with making policy inputs at both national and regional levels.

A brief outline of the campaign's history and objectives, set out in its own terms

The Campaign for Family Housing (CFH) emerged (as the campaign itself explained) in 1977 as 'an informal association of London community and action groups, meeting from time to time, to discuss common problems, and campaigning together on specific issues in the Campaign for Family Housing.' The two main areas of concern, which were emphasised in a letter explaining the campaign to potential member organisations, were the 'problems raised by the high cost of land for housing in Central London, and mutual support by members of the Campaign at each other's lobbies, public inquiries, etc.'. The goals of the campaign, as expressed at this period, focused upon:

(a) increasing 'the residential population in Central London communities through the development of family housing by redevelopment, conversion and rehabilitation – this accommodation to be available at low rents';

(b) halting 'commercial developments such as offices, office conversion and hotels on sites and in buildings where family housing is needed by the community';

  (c) changing 'planning policies so that social need is the basis
      for planning the use of land and buildings instead of profit.'

In other words, the key issue was posed as this – could working-
class communities survive in Central London? While the core of
the group's member organisations came together initially to offer
each other mutual support and information, the group also
developed a lobbying function, feeding in alternative policy
proposals, based upon the direct experience of the local member
community groups.

These contacts between community organisations centred
initially upon the Riverside groups in North Southwark, Battersea,
and then Waterloo, coming together to share experiences and to
offer each other mutual support around a series of major planning
inquiries. For example, North Southwark Community Development group went to a major planning inquiry in 1974 to support
the Battersea Riverside Action Group in making their case for
developing the site to provide jobs and housing for the local
working-class community, rather than for offices to extend the
service functions of the City of London, as the developers were
proposing (for the Morgan Crucible site).

The contact between community groups, at this initial stage,
then, offered shared learning experiences and opportunities to
pool planning expertise (including procedural competence, in
presenting the case to maximum effect at the public inquiries), as
well as offering more general support and solidarity. From an
early phase, CWS was involved in some back-up and support
work to these community groups.

By 1977, these initial and somewhat sporadic contacts became
rather more formalised. This was, in part at least, in direct
response to the overall political situation at that time with
potential changes both in local government elections in the
following year, and possibly at central government level, too,
within the next couple of years. According to this perspective, the
relative quiescence of the property development market (since the
previous boom had burst in 1974) was unlikely to last much
longer. The Labour government of the day was, the groups felt,
deficient enough in its analysis of the probable impact of these
changes upon working-class communities in Central London. The
1977 White Paper on the inner cities was symptomatic of those

shortcomings, demonstrating, these activists argued, insufficient understanding of the contradictions, for example, between increased office space and speculative office and hotel developments on the one hand, and the competing pressures for working-class/family housing and jobs in Central London, on the other. Any changes in political control would, it was believed, lead to a rapid deterioriation in the prospects of the latter interests to the benefit of the former. In what was widely believed to be a pre-election period, it was felt that the case for the local communities' interests urgently needed to be put (while there was still time), at both local and central government levels.

The campaign's analysis of the major issues appeared in several public documents, including press statements, the paper entitled 'Policy for the inner cities' produced in response to the White Paper bearing the same name in 1977 (the cover of which dramatically illustrated the cracks in official policy) and in their evidence to one of the key public inquiries (Coin Street), germane to these issues, over the period in question. The 'Policy for the inner cities' paper, for example, pointed to the concern of local residents 'at the decline of population associated with the reduction of low-cost family housing and the consequent loss of local shops, schools and other amenities.' 'Many people,' the report continued, 'have left because of slum clearance and redevelopment. Still more homes have been lost to office blocks and motor cars. Land values have soared in the face of "redevelopment potential", so that many remaining housing units have become, in a valuer's terminology, "uneconomic" since they do not maximise "investment potential".'

Yet despite these pressures, the local communities involved in the campaign's constituent organisations wanted to stay in Central London: 'The communities of Central London are alive but hardly well. They do not want to move to Milton Keynes en bloc.' These Inner London communities 'must be supported and encouraged', the report continued, 'by providing them with what they fundamentally need, which is good quality *family accommodation* at low rents!'.

The alternative would be a serious loss of vitality as community services deteriorated, and Central London would be increasingly dominated by office blocks, hotels and occasional 'pieds-à-terre' for the wealthy.

'The Government', commented another campaign paper written in December 1978,

> had continually made references to the dereliction of Inner City areas. The areas are composed of living communities that are under extreme pressure. . . . The Campaign for Family Housing is primarily concerned that these areas be provided with the housing they need, in the areas where people live and want to continue living, at rents that they, the ordinary people, can afford. However, these areas are being surrendered either indirectly through councils pursuing commercial interests or directly through commercial initiative gaining council approval.

The campaign was not proposing that housing need was the only problem, nor indeed suggesting that meeting this need was the only solution required for the inner city. The group specifically welcomed, for example, the inner cities White Paper's proposals for industrial development. (At least one of the groups was pressing for land to be used for industrial development as well as for low-cost housing.) It was specifically commercial development and speculation which were identified as the forces 'destroying our communities'.

Starting as they did, from their various experiences in their local communities, the member organisations came to share an increasingly explicit common framework, in face of the increasing pressures represented by the twin forces of political changes at GLC and then the national levels, and the renewed wave of investment in commercial properties, hotels, etc. (as the property market began albeit hesitantly to recover from the 1974 down-turn).

The campaign organisation develops

Over the course of 1978, the Campaign for Family Housing began to put its own internal organisation on a more regularised and systematised basis and expanded its contacts, both in London and more widely nationally.[8]

In the summer of 1978, for example, the campaign drew up a letter containing its analysis of the problem and its objectives to circulate to eleven other potential member groups (five of these

groups did become actively involved in the campaign eventually).
'To be effective', this letter emphasised, 'an association will need
regular broad-based support from groups in Inner London,' on the
basis of an organised lobby to press for alternative policies, as well
as combining the need for the more informal information
exchange and mutual support network.

The possibility of acquiring a full-time worker was also
discussed at this point, a further indication of the group's
increasing formalisation (although it was agreed eventually that
this proposal was premature, and in the event, funds proved
elusive in the more stringent climate of the public expenditure
cuts). The campaign was by this time, however, receiving some
crucial back-up support via CWS.

While the campaign was reorganising itself over this period, it
remained as a clearly specified objective that the group was still a
federation, operating from a local community-based mandate,
rather than a more hierarchically organised regional pressure
group; although in practice, there would nevertheless seem to have
been considerable tensions inherent in this commitment to being a
loosely knit network accountable to local communities, on the one
hand, and an effective lobbying force on the other (as some of the
informants themselves explained).

Even so, this lobbying process was, in its own terms, relatively
successful initially. Despite certain setbacks from relevant politicians when in government, the campaign succeeded in presenting
arguments which were subsequently incorporated in policy
documents at regional (i.e., GLC) and national levels – at least by
politicians in opposition.

Certain campaign members actually commented on this very
problem when attempting to evaluate their success in lobbying for
policy changes. In other words, while they felt positively about the
impact which they seemed to have been making on policy
discussions (in the Tribune Group, the regional and town planning
committee of the Labour Party nationally and the Labour Party at
GLC level, for example), they recognised that the inclusion of
policy recommendations in a political manifesto, for instance, is,
in itself, no guarantee of these proposals' implementation.

Even so, with all these limitations, the group still felt overall
that the lobbying process had represented some achievement.
Policy alternatives had been lodged on the political agenda both at

national and local levels, based directly upon the experiences of local community struggles – a move, if still only a modest one, towards opening up political decision-making processes to a wider democratic discussion.

The lobbying process continued at national and GLC levels (the campaign made an input into the 1980 Labour Manifesto discussions, urging the GLC to adopt 'as a primary aim an increase in the amount of low-rise family housing for rent in and around the centre of London in order to provide support for existing communities and to provide accommodation for service workers and their families, through using the GLC's housing planning and land requisition process to the full and seeking special funds to do so.'

At national level in the spring of that year, there was a meeting for a campaign press release to launch a new publicity attempt to 'Save our Cities', attended by MPs (including front bench Labour representatives) who were broadly sympathetic to the campaign's aims. Furthermore, campaign members were invited to submit proposals on planning policies to the Labour Party Town and Country Planning Committee for September that year, i.e., 1980.

In addition to presenting their case for the defence of working-class communities in Inner London through these alternative policy formulations, the Campaign for Family Housing took part in a major and highly symbolic debate on these issues at a public inquiry in 1979. This was the Coin Street inquiry, which involved the possible re-zoning of the Coin Street site in Waterloo, from 'a substantial emphasis on low cost housing and restraint on office growth [in the local District plan] towards, in contrast, a private office/commercial development'. The site was located within one of the member organisation's communities, and bordered on that of another. As a joint statement by these local communities explained, 'Waterloo does not need offices, oil company head-quarters or hotels. But it *does* need family houses and open spaces. . . . Waterloo is the test case for Inner City regeneration.'

The Campaign for Family Housing was enabled to treat the Coin Street inquiry as a test case and to put considerable resources into collating evidence from the different (and from new) groups, because at this time a new worker was appointed at CWS. Up to this time, CWS had tended to support the campaign through the provision of general back-up services, such as the provision of a meeting place, whereas now a major element in the new CWS staff member's work-load was allocated to support for the campaign. So, although CFH did not have their own paid worker, as they had begun to press for, they did have considerably greater organisational and research resources at their disposal.

The community groups' perspective on the Coin Street issues could, therefore, be put fully and carefully – and with much attendant publicity. In the event, the minister accepted the inspector's view that the developers' proposals be rejected, which was at least a temporary victory for the local working-class community organisations (although the developers subsequently presented a revised version of their plans, so that the initial victory was only one battle in a more protracted war). It was a battle which had considerable symbolic significance, all the same, for community groups in London and more widely.

The broader housing campaigning

So far, the discussion has focused upon the Campaign for Family Housing's role in terms of alternative policy formulation and the public presentation of community groups' perspectives on housing and planning issues in Inner City London. As well as acting as a mutual support network for each member group, however, the campaign did also take part in initiatives to build a broader organisation around these issues. For example, over the spring and summer of 1978, CFH were involved in the organisation of two very successful workshop/conferences on the Inner City – the Inner City Alliance meetings in May and September 1978. The attendance included groups from outside London (such as from Birmingham, Coventry and Cardiff). As the report of the first meeting explained, 'the workshop concluded with a general agreement that the day had been a great success,' in terms of exchanging information, experiences and ideas.

While no permanent organisational links emerged from these two meetings, the contacts formed one strand in the subsequent development of the Housing Liaison Committee, to which the campaign affiliated early in 1980. This represented a more systematic attempt to unite different community and Labour-movement-based housing organisations and struggles, nationally.

More recent developments in London

Subsequently, the CFH reconstituted itself as the Campaign for Homes in Central London. This change of title had been discussed as early as 1978, and represented the inclusion of the interests of groups who were campaigning, too, for single people in London (represented in considerable proportion in Paddington/Westminster, for example) as well as for family housing per se. The change of name also coincided with a new wave of activity (symbolised by the 'Save our Cities' poster campaign 'to stop the new property boom from wiping out the last remaining residential communities in the City Centre. . . . We do not need more offices in Central London, since the combined effects of office relocations and the new microchip technology is likely to make many existing Central London offices redundant within 15 years. . . . In 10 years, Central London will be a ghost town unless we build more homes now.'

Another potentially significant feature of this phase was the renewed emphasis upon forging links with the trade union movement. A joint meeting was planned, plus a campaign exhibition at Congress House, the Trades Union Congress headquarters.

As it has been suggested already, however, there were certain inherent tensions between the community organising and the lobbying approaches (and, inevitably, there were some differences of perspective amongst the member organisations, not least because each community group had been organised round its own specific problems with its own particular structure and approach).

On the one hand, the lobbying and the alternative policy-making was justified precisely because these policies arose from the direct experience of the communities themselves. Several of the respondents clearly put considerable store by the fact that Campaign for Family Housing/Homes in Central London was founded upon respect for the principle that ideas must originate from the communities themselves, rather than from any paid 'experts' – 'starting from where people are,' as one respondent put it, 'rather than from where any professionals thought they ought to be.' Some members, on the other hand, saw potential tensions, for example, between a lobbying and a community development approach, fearing that the former might lead to a small number of activists becoming increasingly distanced from the communities at risk.

This problem was potentially exacerbated when member community groups had paid workers, who were, of course, available during the day, to answer press inquiries, for example, when the local members were at work. The CWS support worker was generally agreed, however, to have been sensitive to this problem, and to have been careful to resist the daily pressures to become a spokesperson and to provide leadership himself. In the evaluation interviews, there was even some criticism that he had been too reticent in this respect, from some of the groups most committed to pressing ahead with the campaigning side of the work.

Postscript

Subsequently, the Campaign for Family Housing/Homes in Central London's involvement with the policy-making process was taken significantly further, following the election of the Labour GLC in 1981. The new planning committee embarked on a major policy initiative, the 'Community Areas Policy'. In this, the GLC's approach to planning started from challenging the 'effect that private enterprise has had on the destruction of local communities'. In response, the newly elected GLC committed itself to devising programmes to identify areas of 'Inner and Outer London with a predominantly working class population where development sites are needed for new housing, community facilities and industry for the benefit of the local community, where these sites are either under pressure for commercial development or are blighted for any other reason.' For such 'community areas', the GLC would develop strategic policies, together with the direction of funds from the development budget 1982-3 and succeeding years, to promote the type of development which *would* meet the needs of the existing residents and workforce.[9] This paper on community areas policy was agreed in March 1982, after a consultation phase which involved the groups which made up the Campaign for Family Housing/Homes in Central London together with the London boroughs, London-wide organisations including the South-east region of the TUC and the London Chamber of Commerce and Industry and a wide selection of community groups and interested individuals.

The first areas selected for particular attention included Spitalfields, South Bank and Fitzrovia, as well as South Hackney, Hammersmith and Southall.

The Campaign for Family Housing/Homes in Central London, meanwhile, was preparing to play an expanded role in the consultation process, and in the implementation of community areas policy, preparations which included the revival of the proposal to seek funding for their own worker. This was to continue the developing dialogue between community groups in these areas threatened by market development pressures, both individually and through their joint organisation CFH/Homes in Central London, on the one hand, and the policy-makers, feeding directly into the political process, on the other.

SWAPAC and the South Wales Association of Tenants (SWAT) – comparisons and contrasts

The second example of resource centre housing work focuses, in contrast, upon local campaigning rather than upon campaigning in relation to alternative policy formulation. In particular, this example deals with the process of organisation-building itself and the effects of involvement in building a tenants' federation upon the consciousness of the key activists themselves. The case in point was the formation of a federation of tenants' groups in South Wales (South Wales Association of Tenants/SWAT), with the support of one of the community workers from SWAPAC. The community workers and the tenants themselves provided the basis for the following account, for the evaluation process, illustrating their concern with developing an immediately relevant and non-sectarian practice which was also radical in its longer-term implications.

Origins and development of SWAT and its relationship to SWAPAC

The key presenting problems which sparked off the initiatives to form SWAT focused upon housing maintenance in the public sector and specifically upon the issues of heating and dampness.

Ironically, perhaps, though by no means uniquely, faulty, ineffective and expensive heating systems and damp were not confined to the older estates at all, emerging, too, on some of the newer public housing estates in the area.

For the tenants, poor heating and dampness were creating unbearable living conditions. The tenants were also typically concerned about the adverse effects of the damp upon their own and especially their children's health (for example, their increased proneness to chest infections). In addition, these ineffective heating systems were very expensive to run. Tenants ran the risk of amassing debts very rapidly, with all the consequent attendant dangers (e.g., of having their electricity cut off and/or falling into rent arrears, thus facing possible eviction). Housing maintenance problems were, then, intimately bound up with a range of other problems, material, physical and social.

The initial trigger to the process of SWAT's development came from the success of one particular tenants' group in resolving these issues. This is how SWAT has explained its own origins and developments:

In January 1979, after two years of persistent campaigning, a group of tenants on Glyntaff Farm Estate near Pontypridd, finally succeeded in persuading Taff Ely Council to change the heating system in their homes from electricity to gas. Up to this point, electricity bills for a winter quarter were anything up to £250, yet even these sums were not providing adequate heating. The new gas system was both cheaper and more effective.

Success meant that many of the 1,000 parents and children involved no longer faced the choice, as they put it, between

freezing or incurring mounting debt, between buying food or buying more clothes, between giving their children Christmas presents or offering them a better diet than chips and baked beans. It meant that hot water would come out of the taps and there was an end to children being permanently on antibiotics – summer as well as winter – to cure their damp-induced infections.

Above all, it meant that people were no longer forced to live in poverty simply because they lived in council houses with expensive, yet inadequate heating systems – council houses which were paradoxically financed by the state as one means of ensuring that people had access to decent housing, but housing that they could not afford to run.

But success, the organisers explained, led to something else, too:

> the tenants involved in this campaign came to realise that they had gained a great deal of experience. They also realised that there were many other groups of tenants in South Wales with similar sorts of problems. So they decided to try and make their experiences available to other tenants, to help other tenants in their campaigns and to work towards linking these different groups together into a federation.

> Within 18 months, this one successful group from Glyntaff Farm Estate, assisted by tenants from the other estates that they had helped, together created the organisation known as South Wales Association of Tenants. Some 16 groups scattered around throughout South Wales had been formed or advised by these tenants, drawing on their own experiences in fighting campaigns for better housing.

Some of this total of sixteen groups won their campaigns very rapidly and then disbanded, not remaining in existence long enough to become a part of SWAT. By mid 1980, about eight groups were playing an active part in building SWAT, however, even though some of them had already won the campaigns on their own estates. In other words, these groups were contributing to the work of SWAT, to support others, not for any particular immediate benefit for themselves:

> So far, there have been important practical achievements, two major campaigns have been won in addition to the one at Glyntaff Farm. At Penarth in the Vale of Glamorgan district, the council agreed to convert a central heating system from electricity to gas on an estate of 350 flats. At the Graig in the Afan Valley district, the council agreed to insert new damp proof courses, to carry out major repairs, to redecorate externally and to insulate the houses even though they had been

the subject of major (although ineffective) rehabilitation work only 8 years previously.

In addition, a number of councils have agreed to carry out both minor repairs and major improvement programmes at a later date, or have changed their policies as a result of the work of SWAT. Already several thousand people are living in warmer, drier homes. Their health has improved and they have a greater disposable income. These, then, are some of the concrete achievements that can be measured after 18 months.

SWAT believed that there were some equally important, if less tangible developments that can be identified, too, as they explain thus:

For the most active tenants, their campaigns and the growth of SWAT has been a vitally important learning experience. They have learnt a greater self-confidence, self-esteem and self-awareness. They have learnt about housing issues to the point where they can take an informed part in local and national policy debates for the first time.

They take a greater interest in the schooling of their children. They take a greater interest in current affairs and they develop a thirst for education. Some have already obtained places as mature students on a full-time course starting in September 1980.

In short, they have become more active participants in society and 'the democratic process than at any other period of their lives.'

And they were doing so in ways, SWAT believed, which promised permanently to reverse the patterns of inequality and marginalisation in society that lead to poverty and under-privilege. 'As an organisation, SWAT attaches equal importance to both these major aspects of its work; the improvement of living conditions and material circumstances on estates and the personal and collective development of individual tenants.'

These twin objectives have had an important bearing on how SWAT has organised itself:

Its [SWAT's] approach has been based on tenants working with tenants as opposed to simply community workers working with or for tenants. Tenants from different groups are regularly in touch with each other. At the weekly meetings of each group, tenants from other areas attend. If one group decides to lobby its council it calls upon other groups to support it.

These organisational contacts are reinforced at regular social evenings organised by SWAT which draws groups together from many parts of South Wales. SWAT also co-ordinates the arrangements for its member groups to attend national conferences and has organised exchange visits with other tenant groups in the Midlands and the North East of England. 'Guy Fawkes' parties were arranged for the children on the various estates and a pantomime was written by the tenants to tour the different estates at Christmas 1980.

These activities are planned at regular monthly SWAT meetings of delegates from each of the groups. As the organisers explained, 'everyone is kept informed of progress in the different campaigns of the member groups. It is here too that overall policy matters are discussed, and local conferences organised when the need has arisen.' Public health consultancy and access to legal advice have also been available to the groups through SWAT.

SWAT, then, has developed rapidly over the last two to three years, covering a large, and typically, internally, inaccessible region in South Wales, where particular estates have been isolated and previously unable to participate in any such broader-based organisation. While SWAT believes that it has encountered many difficulties and made mistakes, the organisation also believes that it has learnt from these, and emerged stronger through the process.

The evaluation interviews

The evaluation interviews (with individual tenants) in 1980 substantially confirmed SWAT's self-evaluation, although it must also be added that the interviews did inevitably leave gaps, on some aspects of the processes involved. In particular, the role played by SWAPAC did not emerge sufficiently clearly from the interviews with the tenants. This, the organisers believed, reflected a genuine uncertainty about the nature of SWAPAC for most tenants, which, they felt, reflected SWAPAC's approach to working with client groups: 'Put simply, SWAPAC believes firmly that its function is to support and improve the effectiveness of the organisation it works for rather than working explicitly for SWAPAC's own image.'

In the case of the work with SWAT, SWAPAC provided the following resources:

— seconded a member of SWAPAC's staff to work full-time as SWAT's organiser and in a way which was accountable to the tenants in SWAT directly;
— provided financial support to meet some of the considerable travelling costs involved in tenants moving around South Wales and attending conferences nationally. As the tenants were all on low wages, these important interactions would not have taken place without financial support, at this stage.
— provided legal advice to groups through SWAPAC's staff member who was a solicitor and provided the consultancy fee to employ a public health consultant to advise groups on their statutory rights and the procedures to adopt and enforce them.

Understandably, in these circumstances, as the organisers explain themselves:

the full-time worker seconded to SWAT (referred to in the interviews as Mike) was identified by many tenants as working with SWAT rather than SWAPAC. A further confusion arose because members of SWAPAC management committee (including 'Barbara') worked alongside 'Mike' with the tenants but in a voluntary capacity.

The role played by these three 'non-tenants' involved striking a balance between helping tenants to develop and express their own skills and organising abilities and assuming key positions for short periods when, for example, particular campaigns reached a crucial stage of development. For the most part, however, they played administrative and enabling roles servicing the individual campaigns or the SWAT organisation and providing the means of transport for tenants to travel to meetings, facilitating rather than directing SWAT's development.

It would appear that their roles expanded, too, on occasions, beyond the provision of such a low-key administrative support, when the need arose. For example, several tenants referred to Mike and Barbara as sources of 'moral support', to assist in the resolution of internal problems when there were conflicts between different members of the group. 'We are emotional vampires, really, we drain them,' commented one tenant in this context.

But one of the organisers' more important functions, they believed, was to identify (through other community workers or SWAPAC's contacts) estates where tenants needed help. Without this network of contacts it would not have been possible for SWAT to develop so rapidly.

It became clear from the interviews that this contact and intelligence network of SWAPAC was indeed a crucial factor, first in making contact with the Glyntaff Farm campaign, and then in enabling the tenants involved in this to expand their links with other groups. Moreover, these links could not have been established if SWAPAC had been unable also to provide financial support for travelling.

A tenant from the Glyntaff campaign explains how this process operated on his own estate:

'Well, we started the Action Group because we were all experiencing very high fuel bills on this estate [a modern estate with electric central heating]. We began to realise that other people on the estate were in the same position. We felt that the fuel bills left us with no money – no money at all. So, we tried going round knocking on doors to tell the other tenants that there would be a meeting. In fact, it proved a great problem to find a place to have the meeting, though. The authorities wouldn't give us the local school and they wouldn't give us the Labour Club. They blocked us. So, we had meetings in a tenant's house. But people weren't coming – although we had a series of these meetings. We went on for about a year like that.

'Then SWAPAC got in contact with us, although we didn't know of them beforehand. I think Mike came first. He offered to lend us enough money to hire a bus for our next meeting. So we put leaflets through the doors of the estate saying that there would be a bus leaving the Labour Club at 7 pm for the meeting. And, luckily because we put the free bus on, about fifty people attended and the council really started taking notice of us. At that point, then, we really started becoming an effective organisation. It showed us what both communication and money meant.

We started our own money then, but it was costing us nearly £20 for a bus. Well, £20 would take us months to raise. It was hard work.

SWAPAC were very helpful to us, in other ways, too, apart from the initial finance to launch us. They told us about social security and about our rights as council tenants. That has been very useful really, because when I go round to see people and they have problems with social security, I can help them now. Or I can phone up Terry [one of the welfare rights workers in TAU] at SWAPAC, if I don't know the answer and get the information for them.'

Similarly, the Graig tenants (who were put in touch with SWAT by a student community worker in June 1979) felt that SWAT's role through SWAPAC had been crucial in their campaign:

'I don't think anyone had thought of having a tenants' association here before. We wouldn't have had one if we had not had outside support. We were concerned about the damp, of course, but we just put up with it. We had to put up with it before these people from SWAT came along. They put us on our way, you know, advised us how to go about things.

'Without Mike and Ashley [from another tenants' group] and their group as well, we wouldn't have got anywhere at all. We used to have meetings with them, once or twice a week. A public health inspector inspected the houses and he said that the problem wasn't condensation [as the council were claiming], but that it was definitely rising damp. He looked at every house. After that we pushed and pushed the council and now we have had a lot done and the council have spent several thousand pounds on these houses since then. Now that we've won, even the councillors admit that it was really damp and not condensation.'

The isolation of groups in South Wales, because of the particular geographical pattern of mountains and settlements, combined with the underprovision of community work resources and agencies, comes out very clearly, too, in the case of the Graig:

'We wouldn't have done it without them. We wouldn't even have had any money for bus fares and so on.'

Finally, as a further evaluation of the relevance of SWAPAC's support role via SWAT, the tenants were asked what they felt the effect on their organisation would be if SWAPAC's assistance were no longer available. On the one hand, there was a unanimously expressed view that SWAT would not have become an effective organisation without SWAPAC's support. But on the other hand, there were also expressions of hope that part at least of SWAT's work was now self-sufficient enough to continue, although clearly the present momentum would be hard to sustain.

Q. 'What do you think would be the effect on your groups and other groups if the funding and support you get from SWAPAC came to an end?

A. 'Well, it would create problems. None of us have any money to spare. We're all very poor and if it wasn't for SWAT, we wouldn't have got anywhere. They've got us to places that we could never have got to. If it wasn't for SWAT we'd be just where we were when we started.'

But, as another tenant explained:

'If SWAPAC went and with it the support for SWAT, I hope that the work with tenants would carry on, though. It should do to some extent, but we do need money. If we had no money at all in SWAT except for the money that the tenants could raise themselves, we couldn't do everything we are doing now.'

Another group expressed a similar sense of strong committment:

'We would still be involved in SWAT and helping other groups in other places. I feel that even if we can't help ourselves, perhaps we can help others. I feel we've got something to offer from what we've learned.'

SWAT and SWAPAC appear to have offered some kind of 'security', too, the organisers believed:

'To be honest, my wife and I are still sometimes both frightened. I think that part of the education process in SWAT, an important part, is that we know what rights we've got now, though I am still a bit fearful of councillors. I keep wondering if they can evict me. But while SWAPAC is there, I feel more confident because I know I can get legal advice – that's a bit of security.'

As the organisers have already emphasised in their account of SWAT's overall goals and strategies, ends and means were explicitly and inextricably bound together. The aim was to support the tenants in achieving concrete and immediate improvements in their housing conditions, while at the same time facilitating a broader and longer term process of community education, on the tenants' own terms, ultimately defined and controlled by them, not by the organisers, let alone SWAPAC. So, as they explained:

the link between the tactics that won campaigns and also helped those involved to achieve greater self-confidence and personal development was something that emerged out of the experiences of the tenants themselves at Glyntaff Farm Estate.

It is important to recognise, too, that this approach to campaigning was adopted by this tenants' group *before* SWAPAC made contact with it. Having won their campaign on the strength of these tactics, it was the tenants' own experience which led them to advocate this approach to those other groups which they subsequently helped to form. SWAPAC did not seek to influence groups in shaping their approach to campaigning, either when it was providing support to the Glyntaff Farm group or subsequently when this group started to build the organisation that became South Wales Association of Tenants.

The tenants themselves explained this process, which led them to draw certain lessons from their experiences, and adopt a particular form of tactics. Key elements in these tactics have encompassed the use of direct action to surprise and embarrass the relevant authorities, and the adoption of tactics which generate a sense of solidarity and strength, mutual support and confidence together with a sense of fun and *joie de vivre*, typified by the use of songs:

'I suppose we ought to start explaining our tactics by discussing our heating campaign really. We started in the usual way with petitions and writing letters, and we were more or less ignored by the council; we were disregarded actually, and even called educationally sub-normal. When the letters and petitions didn't work we sat down one day and said, "what we ought to do is to chain ourselves to the railings," and the next thing is, we did it! We chained ourselves to the railings for 24 hours and the police brought us blankets in the night and the railway men brought us tea. It was incredible. The press came, the television people came, and suddenly – as a result – even our councillors greeted us. Then we realised that this was the key, this militant direct action.

'We got together again later on and decided we would have a march. And we occupied the council offices and took over one of their meetings and all the councillors made a dash for the door. They were all nervous, you know, and I looked at them and thought: "you ought to feel how nervous I am."

'There was always this bluff, you know. We kept marching and so on and in the end the councillors agreed that we had a problem. But even then they said that although they sympathised they didn't have the money to solve our problems. So they gave us, as an emergency measure, calor gas fires. We had these fires and we thought: "Oh, they've given us a fire, that's marvellous." We were so grateful. But we were still cold and the condensation was still there. We had damp really badly and it was that bad winter in 1978. We all felt that we couldn't bear to see our children suffering. They were so cold, especially in the night, and it was antibiotics, antibiotics, because they were always ill.

'Eventually, we said that we'd had a belly-full. It didn't

matter if they arrested us. So we took deckchairs and flasks of tea and toys into the council offices and we sat down and we started singing. It was total chaos.

'The Mayor came and asked how could we do this. We should be ashamed. Anyway, he said they would have an emergency meeting, which they did have. It was a terribly difficult meeting, because they really tried to put us down. Anyway, two weeks later, after that meeting, they agreed to convert us to gas heating. We were really over the moon for joy. We thought it was incredible that we had won.

'We decided then we had so much energy (after the two years campaigning in all that it had taken us to win this victory), that we decided to form an association of tenants, made up from different groups, to tell other tenants about the short-cuts we had used when we were campaigning and what we had learnt from the process. The first group we contacted was in Penarth, and we met together and talked about tactics and everything. They won in a very short time as a result. And we've been fighting with another group, too. They live in Abergwyni, and their houses are just terrible, but we've almost won there, too. But it was only through our SWAT tactics. Wherever we go we sing songs and make a noise because councils don't seem want to listen to reason alone. Letters, petitions alone don't get us anywhere.'

Another tenants' group echoed the same lessons of the appropriate moment for changing from negotiation to direct action, together with the use of 'unreasonableness':

'Well, we were living in the same sort of conditions, we had electric blower central heating with vents in the ceilings, so we had hot heads and cold feet! We had condensation and damp and we put up with it for about 10 years. Then, when people complained the council gave us permission to install our own gas central heating which would have cost £1,000 a time. That was the straw which broke the camel's back, really. So we thought, "that's it; damn cheek!"

'I went out with a friend to get a petition signed and Glantaff came down to see us. Meanwhile we got the same old story from the council – they said it was our own fault and that they could do nothing for us — they had no money and that we weren't using the heating properly anyway. It was just ridiculous. So, then we tried different tactics. We started disrupting council meetings and organising demonstrations. It took Glantaff two years to win their campaign. It took us only six months.'

This unreasonableness stemmed initially from anger. As one woman said:

'It was putting the kids to bed in cold that made us really angry. It overcame everything, this anger.'

But the women soon began to realise how their anger, even their hysteria could be useful, too, in putting over their point of view and compelling councillors and officials to take some real notice of their problems. For certain situations the children, whom the women had formerly regarded as an encumbrance, could be a useful weapon, too, and the children also helped people to enjoy the demonstrations:

'We did a demonstration on the steps of the Welsh Office in the summer. Ironically, it was the summer when we were complaining about being freezing cold! The tenants got dressed in nightclothes with woollen hats and hot-water bottles, saying this was how they had to go to sleep . . . the kids were great. They kept us going when we were passing out from the heat. They were running around cheering everyone up and that. It was a really joyful occasion.'

Another tactic which was frequently utilised was simply to do a stunt, to gain publicity:

'We don't use the same tactics twice, though. If we do a thing once, then another time we'll try and do something different. Once, we got a Wendy House and we got inside it and we marched. It seems that if you go sensibly dressed you get ignored but if you go as Noddy, they'll listen.'

Whether they have used this type of direct action, or whether they have used non-direct legal tactics, the tenants have often met with hostility from authorities, however:

'We have started to use legal action against certain councils as we have some proof, in *their* own terms, that what we are saying is right. But they're saying that we are being very rude and irresponsible to resort to legal action. For example, in Penarth, where a couple of the families have written to the council saying that they are going to claim damages, the council have written back to say that they will claim counter damages against the tenants for not keeping the house properly.'

To their surprise, however, the tenants have always found the police helpful and reasonable, which they have appreciated.

'The police have been very nice. Whenever we've marched we've never come across any police harassment. I think we're lucky mind! They could have taken a harder line. But, maybe because we're housewives, they're lenient. Even when the council officials say to the police "get these people out of here," the police refuse. In the sit-in, they actually let us back in again. I think women can get away with more than men. If we'd been men I think we would have been arrested, but because we were women the police just laughed. The police were great, in the last sit-in when we stayed for three nights and locked all the doors.'

The groups also gave each other more self-confidence, an aspect which SWAT believes is particularly crucial. The impact of the mutual support which was involved in groups working together was described by one of the tenants, as follows:

'Other groups have given support and advice. We wouldn't have had the nerve to demonstrate without them. And in the sit-in they brought us meals, chicken and things . . . they've been marvellous.'

Singing is another such mechanism for developing mutual self-confidence:

'Songs are very important to us. We write a new one for every campaign. When we're feeling bad they make us feel better. They get the adrenalin going, you know. People had songs in battles years ago. Take Maria, for instance, sometimes she can't say things, but she can sing them!'

> On top of the Graig
> all covered in mould,
> we're always so sick
> we're always so cold.
> The little kids shiver
> the old people die,
> come see our houses
> then you will know why.
> Well, the council they told us
> that they understood
> and sent down some workmen,
> if we were good.
> Well, the workmen came,
> and they did their best,
> so Afan council
> could have a good rest.
> The damp and the mould
> it won't go away,
> that's why we've come here
> to tell you today.
> Why must we beg you?
> Why must we shout?
> Oh, Afan council,
> please get us out.

> We are the South Wales Tenants come to London for
>   the day
> We haven't got much money but we've got a lot to say.
> We may be valley dwellers but one thing you ought to
>   know,
> We won't put up with the housing cuts, this Government's
>   got to go.
> And we were singing, hymns and arise,
> land of my fathers.

Now we've been in trouble with the council you should
    know,
We've been cold and damp and miserable and had nowhere
    to go,
But we are all united now – together we will fight,
for better housing is our goal and is our basic right,
And we were singing
Hymns and arise,
land of my fathers.
Ogey, Ogey, Ogey!!!

'That's been part of our tactics, you know, that we always use
songs, because we believe that unless you can put an element of
fun in the work it's just a drag. One of the most important
parts of whatever we've done is that we've had a laugh and a
joke, even though sometimes we've been terribly embarrassed!'

Developing the organisation and mutual support

When the first campaigning group contacted by SWAPAC began
to take direct action, decisions were taken by very few people, on
a spontaneous basis. This spontaneity was seen as an advantage at
first:

'When we said we were going to do the chain-up, for instance,
we thought "Oh, not many people are going to bother us." We
didn't have to answer to many people for what we were doing.
Although we were a small group and we moaned and groaned
about that, it was a good thing in other ways, we thought.
Anyway, its quality, not quantity, that counts, I always said.'

But underlying this spontaneity was the knowledge of the need
for approval or general consensus amongst other tenants of the
estate who had signed the group's petition. So the importance of
feeling that a group had the approval of the estate was realised,
while the difficulties of sustaining a campaign on the strength of a
few group members became, at the same time, clearer.

Other groups gradually came to appreciate the advantages of
more explicit support and the involvement of a wider grouping of
tenants; not only within their own estate but between different
groups:

'Well, I don't think a little committee is any good, really. No
good at all. The whole street should be involved so that you've
got 100 per cent backing all the time. The trouble with us was
that we were just a little committee and I don't think we had
the backing. You see, the tenants were afraid of the council,
afraid of what the council might do. No, the whole street has
got to be involved. Then you're really strong. When you have a
meeting, you want the whole lot to be at that meeting, so that
everybody knows what's going on and they can put their views
to the meeting. When you are just a few and you have to work
it out between you, the others may say then: "No, the group's
decision is wrong." If they're there and they all know what you
are doing, they can't say it's wrong.

'You need the support of others too. That's how it should
be, all backing one another, all fighting together. The more
backing you've got, the better chance you've got with the
council.

'They treat you better if you stand up to them. If you stand
back and just take what they're willing to give, that's what
you'll get. But if you're willing to stand up and fight them,
you'll get treated better, see. You get better respected. But not
everyone understands this. A lot of people have been terrified.
If you live in a council house you're afraid because always in
the back of your mind there's the fear of having gone too far –
that you're going to be evicted – that they're going to get at you
and I can totally understand why some people don't want to
get involved.

'One mistake we did make at first was that we didn't
understand those who didn't want to take militant action. We
effectively said "If you don't want to take militant action you
can just get lost!" But I think we make a mistake there, because
we could have involved those people in other activities. But we
were so committed to militant action that we couldn't
understand how anyone else couldn't be.'

Subsequently, there was greater attention to finding the tactical
pace which would win and develop the broadest organisational
support. Mutual solidarity was seen as crucial to this process. As
one tenant commented:

'What's amazed me since joining SWAT is how, when there is a real issue, people will get out and fight. When the tenants go along and talk about their successes and what they've done, it really gets through to groups. Outside community workers just don't seem to get across to tenants in the same way.

'The idea of the tenants' movement is that you're not on your own anymore. Suppose there was a meeting or a demonstration in one place, for instance, we'd get a coach load of people from the other estates to come and support them.'

As the organisation developed there were more attempts to develop democratic structures within SWAT, with more formally organised meetings, for example:

'You know, we had a monthly meeting in Cardiff when we talked about the structure of SWAT; it helped to feel more involved and we heard everyone's problems.'

As it has already been emphasised, alongside meetings, demonstrations, conferences and so on, SWAT also learned the value of social and cultural events in encouraging and involving the broadest possible range of tenants in the organisation. As another tenant explained about the socials:

'They give us a chance to meet other people and discuss problems. Not only that, though. We've taken what I would call "strangers" from our street to them, people who've never been on a protest march or anything and they've come back with the general idea of what's going on and they know what they've been missing out on. They are more with us now. We get together and we have socials. All the groups come. It's very important, that. It's no good being too heavy, we've found you need to make tenants' groups' work a laugh, too.'

Solidarity and mutual support also involved more difficult learning experiences too, on occasions. For example, SWAT tenants have from time to time felt the need to debate issues with other groups, if they felt that these were offering negative or regressive definitions of their problems. SWAT felt that this ground had to be cleared, however, before a more genuinely collective position could be developed. To take an example:

> 'At one group's meeeting, which was set up to talk about the repairs, a lot of tenants came along and just vented their feelings about the workmen. We [from SWAT] had to tell the tenants that we were very sorry, but if they were going to take that attitude [i.e., blaming the wrong culprit] we were not going to help them at all. At the time they were shocked, but we believed that if they thought about it, they would realise that the workmen are not at fault. The tenants have to see that their problems are not due to faulty workmen, but to the lack of the necessary resources and materials.'

This attitude was part of the attempt to build up solidarity in a broad movement:

> 'It's obvious that you can't win campaigns endlessly unless the government makes sufficient money available. The housing problems won't be solved by councils saying to any one group, "OK – you've embarrassed us up to here, we'll let you have the money for your repairs." Because in the end, if you get enough people doing that they're going to say, "Right, out of the ten of you, we'll give the money to you and you." We have to resist such divisiveness and start thinking more about fighting and getting other people and even councils to join us. We are on the same side, ultimately.'
>
> Q. 'Is that how you're developing, then?'
>
> A. 'Hopefully! Otherwise we're up a gum tree, because if we remain concerned about individual houses or individual estates, then we are going to go on like this for the next 200 years! It's not until we really start looking at national policies and resources that this is going to change. But we can't do that until we have built up more and more groups and become united.'

Developing a broader political awareness

SWAT is convinced that gains have been made in this direction, and that the experience of being involved in their own, and other tenants' campaigns have developed tenants' awareness and understanding of policies and the political process: 'Nobody else could have "taught" them this. It was learning through experience.' As a tenant explained:

'We've all changed in our ideas. How I used to think and how I think now are totally different. If you get somebody coming to you to talk about how you should change your political beliefs, you just think, "Oh, it's another one of them, you know, another politician with his own axe to grind." With us though, this gradual change came through our own experiences. How to explain this change – well, for example, there was a time when you would think, "Oh, a councillor!", but now I think, "Oh, he is just like me, just another person." Actually, he is there because I elected him to be there. I think we've all changed like that.

'At one meeting, we merely clapped when one of our group had spoken, and the chairman of the council started banging his hammer and told us it wasn't a fairground and he would have us evicted. We listened and kept quiet but I was stunned by that meeting. I was always brought up to believe that we lived in a democratic country and before my eyes I watched our council turn the meeting into the Muppet Show; where was the democracy I kept asking myself? I started really thinking, then. Before that I knew nothing at all of local or central government, I never used to read the newspaper, at all. I think differently now.

'As I got involved I gradually realised more and more about life and the mechanisms by which people like myself were branded and put upon and then I realised that the problem that I have myself is all around me too, in the dreary Alcatraz-type flats where I live, where there are 300 other under-privileged people like myself with hang-ups about the council.'

Or, as another tenant explained about the process of political education:

'For example, one of the things that Glantaff people said that they used to believe was that, as long as you voted, that was it. Oh, yes, we used to think that. As long as we had our vote that was all we wanted. No, we hadn't a clue about how councils

worked. We were afraid to go down there in case we got
evicted from our houses.

'Well, we are getting involved in a lot of issues now. It's
seemed to open our eyes to a lot of things. As I said, we've gone
on marches about housing cuts, and so on . . . and broader
issues.

'I've learned that if you've got to fight, then you've got to
fight all the way. I used to see just the council as being the
problem at one time. Now I see that it is the whole system in
which we live. This is something that's come to me gradually.'

But, the process of learning can be very painful, personally. As
another commented:

'It is hard waking up. Sometimes it's hurtful. Like when you
start questioning your political beliefs. That's very painful. I
feel that it's an awakening, but it's also a great disillusionment.
You thought that everything worked out fairly and people were
looked after, and by voting you could get a good government in
and that. Now I know that whoever's in power, they tend to be
out of touch with what's going on. I think that things get done
through work like we do, though.'

Another tenant expressed a similar viewpoint – in relation to the
distance between professionals and working-class clients: 'because
they live in one set of circumstances, they can't identify with
another set. And they talk about council tenants as a race apart.
That is really most disturbing – an indictment of our society.'

So, the motivation to do something for themselves has been
strengthened by the tenants' experiences. As another said:

'I'm a working-class woman who thought that there was no
way I could change my life for the better. Anyway, I thought
my future was safe in the hands of those educated people who
cared about the working class. Then with the Tenants'
Association I started attending conferences and listened to the
marvellous ideas other people have. I was very impressed at
first, but after going to a few more conferences, where people
were saying the same things, which they'd obviously been
saying for the last ten years, and wondering how they would

get the working class involved in wider issues, I realised that
even if much of what they were saying was right, they weren't
living in the same world as me. They didn't realise that most of
the time and energy of the great majority of the working class is
spent in surviving from day to day. We have to work out what
we can do in our own way – on our own terms, not just
because anybody else tells us what to do or think.'

The broadening of issues and areas of concern

The feeling of developing awareness and confidence which grew
out of their experiences has, SWAT believes, helped the tenants to
broaden their understanding and concern with other issues too.
For example, several tenants commented that they seemed to be
responding differently to the coverage of news and events in the
mass media.

'For instance, I notice issues now, on the television that I used
to ignore. There was a programme the other day about flats in
Manchester. We've been to Manchester with the tenants, so I
found that I did understand the issue. So I notice things on the
television and in the papers now, and I discuss them with the
other tenants. If one of us hasn't seen the programme they'll tell
the others. We find we're interested in things now that we
weren't before.

'We would like to do something about other issues now, too,
like unemployment and public transport.'

In the groups which had been involved longer, the feeling had
grown, too, that they had the right to challenge and question a
range of social policies. As one commented, for example:

'There aren't enough facilities here; there are hardly any youth
wings or buildings for youth clubs, nothing for the kids to do.
These new sport centres, supposedly for the community, tend
to be very middle class. I started to go to play badminton, but it
was costing me £1.80 for the two of us, that was each nearly
£1 a morning and you just can't afford that when you're on the
dole, can you? And the people there tend to be very middle
class. They're not really places for the ordinary people and
anyway, it's hard to get a booking.

'I'd specially like to see things done for the very young children. I'd like to see a play centre developed so that mothers could take very young children there for a couple of hours. We were thinking of organising a playgroup, but we've got to have a building. I'd volunteer to help because although my children are quite grown up, I'd like to take younger children off their mother's hands for a bit. The numbers of mothers on tranquillisers on the estate up here – valium and that – is tremendous, not surprising though, living in these kinds of houses, with the kids screaming and that. You see, there's nowhere for the children. It's just concrete mazes.'

The tenants also demonstrated greater confidence that they could actually *do* something about some of these issues. As one group explained:

'They are thinking now about trying to do something here about a community centre. We need somewhere on this estate for people to meet. We've been thinking about approaching our councillors because we feel they respond more to us now. There's a school empty down the bottom, and maybe that could be turned into a community centre. I feel that something is needed here for the children, you know. But it's very hard to get the council to respond, even for a community centre. I didn't know what the word meant two years ago, myself, but now I wish we could get one because it would be fantastic.

'I certainly know much more about my rights than I ever knew before. Really, the big difference is this education through doing. I left school at fifteen and I didn't try any exams. My handwriting was terrible! I used to be ashamed to show it. I never wrote much, you see. I do now, though, and it's improving. There's been a slow process of change with all of us. We're all more confident now about a lot of things.'

This learning process involved groups and individuals in different ways. In particular, the process posed special dilemmas for the women who tended to find that their heightened self-confidence and sense of self-esteem created tensions within the family so that there had to be changes in the balance of their personal relationships. Ultimately, the conclusion which they drew from these re-alignments were positive, however; the women felt that they neither could nor would choose to return to the former status quo.

The feelings of Graig women who had won their housing struggle

'I feel more confident about things. . . . I'm not a bit frightened now. The only time I'm nervous (and I've got to be truthful, haven't I) is when I make a speech down in the council chambers. . . . I think we have learnt a lot. I've done a lot of thinking. I have changed personally – I feel I can do things now, whereas before I used to come home and couldn't be bothered. You know, I think now, "let's go ahead and do something." I think we're all stronger – stronger as a community now.'

Or, as another woman explained:

'I've changed personally too. For instance, I was really dominated by my husband. If he said, "Oh, you can't do that," or "I want a cup of tea," you know, I used to jump to it. Then I met Jean and Maureen, and a couple of other girls and that's when I became involved in the Action Group. That's how I came to chain myself to the railings. There's nothing I wouldn't try to do now – I'm not afraid of my husband anymore, either. Before, when I was watching the TV (which I didn't often do because there was a lot I didn't understand), some issues would come up on the news and I'd think what's all that about? But now, I'll question things on the news, and if I don't agree, I'll argue with my husband about it.

'I was really quiet and shy and if I saw any official knocking on the door I'd go and get my husband. I'd say, "Oh, there's a bloke, can you see to him." When we started the Action Group, I was really nervous about meeting people. My husband used to tell me I was like a mouse and ask me why I didn't stand up for myself. Now he tells me I'm dictatorial and bossy, so you can't win!

'My husband really seems to be more understanding now, though. Sometimes I throw what we at Glantaff call a "wobbly" when I feel I can't cope. I work, you see, till 12, seven days a week, then I have to come home, do my work, cook and clean, see to my husband. If I feel that it's all on top of me now, I say to him, "Well, come on, you can tidy up today or make the beds or something." But he'll say, "Good God, you're not the same woman as you were a year ago. You don't fetch and carry like you used to." "No, and I'm not going to," I tell him, "I'm working." But he accepts it now. Like today, he fetched the children and he now says: "You're a better person for having some independence." '

As another woman explained too, there could be no turning back now:

'I believe that as a person, I have completely changed. I don't put myself under any political banner, perhaps because I am so unsure, but I do know that I think more for myself now, although the transformation is a very gradual one. I have learnt a lot and now my mind is alive and there is a lot more to be learnt. We won our campaign but I couldn't just shut the world out again. I couldn't go back. I have a good idea of what is happening now. The thought of it ending there for me was depressing – I didn't want to be just a housewife without other concerns.

'When I was a little girl, I always felt that I wished I was a boy. I always felt somehow ashamed of being a girl. I don't now. I think I am totally equal. I'm proud of being female – but I can't imagine going back to my life before we started this. What did I used to do? I was just a housewife – then suddenly you find that you are a person.'

In the event, it has been the development of the women's consciousness, and their own growing interest in further education, both formal (three of the women had entered full-time courses by 1982) and particularly informal, that has represented a key outcome from the SWAT experiences. A SWAT Women's Educational Group has been formed, with plans for small groups to study housing, public health and planning law, local government, health, education, the media, poverty and family income. Eventually the aim is for the participants themselves to become involved in developing study sessions with other women. This potential link-up with adult education, both formal and informal, to widen perspectives and to push for new opportunities would seem to represent a broader strand of considerable significance within community work and the women's movement alike.

In summary

Overall, then, in a period of less than two years, the South Wales Association of Tenants had established itself with some eight active member organisations. In practical terms, they had achieved very considerable improvements in the housing conditions on certain estates and they had prevented the accumulation of debts which had been threatening the tenants using the most costly electric heating system. In some cases, the tenants believed that their local councillors were now far more prepared to listen to their problems and respond to their needs. More abstractly, tenants also expressed the view that they, themselves, had undergone a considerable process of change, self-development and 'education' in the broadest sense of the term.

These comments were all the more remarkable in view of the personal circumstances of some of the key tenants. Several seemed to be coping in the face of quite considerable personal difficulties (for example, one was struggling with a problem of ill-health which involved occasional hospitalisation; another was a single parent with a range of practical problems raising her children on her own). It was striking to consider the extent of these tenants' commitment to helping and supporting each other, when their own personal difficulties were taken into account. Such commitment to collective action and solidarity must be another measure of the achievement of the South Wales Association of Tenants.

Meanwhile, as the tenants themselves were increasingly realising, the broader context of national housing policy was changing rapidly. The combined effects of the public expenditure cuts and the 1980 Housing Act and the 1980 Local Government and Planning Act were predicted to result in the reduction of local governments' room for manoeuvre, thereby reducing the possibilities for successful local action around housing issues in the immediate future.

Although tenants' organisations, such as SWAT, were still building their own local bases, and involving their own communities, they were nevertheless forced to take account of these wider processes and to develop appropriate responses. One strand in this broadening process was represented by SWAT's involvement in the Housing Liaison Committee – which brings the discussion back to the first example and the policy inputs from the Campaign for Family Housing/Homes in Central London. Once again, as in Chapter 4 in relation to information, advocacy and community action, it seemed to emerge that resource centres were increasingly grappling with the problem of building creative links between the different aspects and levels of their strategies.

It would seem to be important to emphasise, too, that the ultimate development of progressively orientated community organisations and federations on the one hand, and their closer involvement in the formal political process on the other, in no way represented any negation of the relevance of neighbourhood work per se, nor any sectarian abandonment of the uncommitted, as some of the critics of radical perspectives would seem to have implied (as discussed in Chapter 2). On the contrary, in fact, both case studies emphasised the importance of retaining and developing the neighbourhood base, together with the importance of winning the broadest possible level of active support from local people for a wider and longer-term strategy.

Conclusion
The way forward

In this study we have traced some of the interrelationships between community work, community action, political action, and the broad Labour movement. Over the past decade or so, we have suggested, there have been significant developments, both positive and negative; and even with the harsher political climate of the early eighties there have been gains, however fragile, as well as reverses. The pressures within the Labour Party for constitutional as well as for progressive political changes illustrate precisely the fragility of these gains and the relative under-development, still, of external support mechanisms within the Labour movement and the electorate more generally. The constituency for socialist policies remains to be more widely constructed. The task at the broadest level is, we have suggested, then, to raise socialist values and analysis from being a minority subculture to being the dominant political and social culture. One of the central themes within this book has been the potential of community action, alongside the broad trade union and Labour movement for stimulating the examination of alternative and socialist solutions to the problems of daily living. Even within government-sponsored community programmes, such as the EEC anti-poverty programme, we have shown that local people have become more than ever convinced that poverty, in all its ramifications, will not be removed by these kinds of pilot studies.

At the very least such programmes can help to stimulate a more democratic environment where people are encouraged to have some say in what is happening to them in their everyday lives and to bargain around decision-making at higher levels. More typically, too, when deprived communities in these programmes have become increasingly aware of the forces which impinge upon their disadvantages and reinforce them, their efforts to change their situation have tended to take on a more overtly political slant. Even the notion of co-operation itself has particular potential ideological implications when it occurs within a society that is predominantly individualistic in its established norms and values.

Even so, we have argued that community action can in no way be simply equated with class struggle; community action has not of course been inherently or automatically socialist per se. Nor can community workers or even community activists afford to ignore the need for professional expertise in the service of communities' demands for what are often very short-term gains. On the contrary, the case studies provided a range of examples of the possibilities for developing *links* between such practical information, advice, and resource support on a range of immediate issues *and* the development of longer-term and more recognisably progressive strategies for change.

While it is in no way being suggested, then, that community action can be defined solely or even essentially in terms of its direct relationship with struggles for socialism, it *has* been argued that community struggles have historically contained and still continue to contain relevance for the longer-term task of creating the necessary climate of popular support for alternative (and ultimately recognisably socialist) goals and strategies.

Given recent debates, however, the legitimacy, let alone the key significance of extra-parliamentary struggles for these long-term goals, the significance of community action has not been generally accepted as unproblematic, in these terms.

But, of course, it can be counterposed that it is those who argue that struggles for progressive policies – and ultimately for a socialist society – must be strictly and narrowly confined to the parliamentry sphere who are effectively denying a critical aspect of labour history, and incidentally challenging, too, a longstanding strand in the development of democratic political theory.

The case for the development of an active participatory democracy as a key element in political education, for example, has been argued in the following terms: 'We do not learn to read or write, to ride or swim, by being merely told how to do it, but by doing it; so it is only by practising popular government on a limited scale that the people will ever learn how to exercise it on a larger scale.'[1] This argument was put forward, not in the wake of the 1968 upheavals, but a century earlier, by John Stuart Mill.

There are innumerable examples, too, of extra-parliamentary action, historically, together with arguments for community-based mobilisation to support industrial struggles. 'If it comes to a fight, the people of London will give their backing to the miners. We know that the struggle of the miners is the struggle of the working people everywhere' – which was not a militant's comment on the 1974 miners' strike, but Herbert Morrison's words in 1926![2]

However significant in themselves, parliamentary strategies have not, in fact, monopolised the attention of Labour movement activists; in addition to trade unions' struggles it has of course been a major theme of this book that over the last decade or so, other forms of extra-parliamentary struggles have also assumed particular significance.

As it has already been argued in the first two chapters, while the post-war boom faded into the profitability crisis of the sixties and seventies, there were critical changes, both in social reality and in political and ideological responses to these. The revival of interest in socialist theory from the late sixties, in particular, included, as Chapter 1 outlined, an upsurge of interest in community action and the development of more 'democratic' participatory mechanisms, together with the development of feminism and the development of black consciousness and resistance.

What is being suggested, is that out of common and/or parallel roots from the mid and late sixties have emerged specific extra-parliamentary movements both within the trade union movement (including the white-collar sectors) and outside it. By the very focus of so much of their concerns – with the role of the state and the welfare state in particular – these movements have a critical potential – and potential has to be underlined, because there is, as we have been emphasising, nothing automatic about the process – a potential for re-thinking social policies, along alternative, critical, and indeed more overtly socialist lines.

So what does such a claim mean, both in theory and in practice?

Probably the most obvious example that has emerged, though only touched on in the case studies, has related to the impact of the women's movement, not only for broadening the definition of the political sphere ('the personal is political'), but for challenging certain key assumptions about the welfare state itself. For example, the women's movement has questioned the social security system's reinforcement of women's dependent status, both within the family and at work, and raised the necessity for rethinking a socialist strategy for income maintenance which takes account of women's rights to financial and legal independence.

Similarly, as Chapter 4 outlined, women's health groups have raised key questions about the content and structure as well as the delivery of health care, reinforcing professional (and typically male) control over their dependent patients rather than promoting the most favourable socio-economic context for positive good health.

Black resistance has represented another critical strand and one that has been even less developed in the case studies. For example, black women have struggled against racism in the very structure as well as the delivery of welfare services (campaigns against depo-provera, for example, and forcible sterilisation, or the campaigns against the 'Sin-bins', which replaced ESN schooling for West Indian children), struggles which are located within Sivanandan's essay 'From resistance to rebellion'.[3] Even more obviously, black organisations have been crucial in the development of pressure for democratic community control of the *police*, an increasingly critical issue in the current political climate.

So far it has been suggested, then, that the impact of these movements and the experiences of community-based struggles have been crucial to the ways in which alternative – explicitly SOCIALIST – welfare strategies are being conceptualised and developed. But, as we have already argued, this does not imply that socialist policies will simply 'emerge' out of these movements, or that all that is necessary is for politicians and policy-makers to '*hear*' what the community/client population is saying.

What *is* being proposed is neither to expect socialist policies to emerge, automatically, from any such democratisation process, nor to revert to former ways of ignoring the inputs from community groups; but rather to engage them in a systematic process of critical dialogue. The Guigliano health project, discussed in Chapter 3, for example, was attempting to develop just such a model of dialogue representing neither a passive populism on the one hand, or traditional patron-client relationships on the other, whether the patron is represented by the public authorities in general or even by the local authorities elected on a specific mandate to pursue progressive, socialist policies.

This brings the argument back to the question of public finance for community work and community action programmes. Can community work and community action be stimulated with public support without the negative associations of the programmes of the sixties and seventies? In particular, support for community action has to be divorced from spurious claims to resolve the structural problem of poverty – on the cheap – or from acting as a cut-price substitute for main spending programmes.

Even if such substitution were accepted as a desirable goal – a contradiction in terms of a socialist welfare strategy – experiences to date (including those of the case studies in the EEC anti-poverty programme) would suggest that it is hardly an easily realisable one. Community action may have led to upsurges of voluntary effort, but as the case studies have demonstrated, community action has also led to increased demands upon the welfare state, involving potentially greater public spending. So public support for community action has to be justifiable in its own right, or not at all.

But what about the question of the use of such programmes to develop state incorporation mechanisms (discussed in Chapter 2)? One of the key issues for certain progressive local authorities who are currently engaged in community action support programmes would seem to be precisely this – how can they develop a critical dialogue with community groups and other movements on an alternative model?

At a local level, certain Labour councils have been moving in precisely this direction. From the outset of the 1980s it has become clear, through the work of Labour-controlled authorities, such as the Greater London Council, that quite consciously councils can begin to finance projects that do have radical long-term goals, as well as for significant short-term improvements to be achieved in the local area. Work with tenants' associations, advice centres, organisations representing ethnic minorities, women's groups working on employment and other issues is important and these do need support, in their own right; and as has already been suggested in relation to the case studies, such projects do include some longer-term potential for change. The very process of undertaking this kind of work could also help to develop a more co-operative collective culture and one which has potential importance for the future developoment of alternative strategies for social change.

The key question, then, from the sum of these experiences, would seem to be how far can Labour councils and other progressive organisations support community action, and progressive social movements, in ways which are neither coercive and manipulative (traditional patron-client relations), nor passive and populist? How far can they develop a process of dialogue which is part of the wider construction of the groundswell of popular support for socialist policies (the political education function), and how far can any future radically oriented Labour government take up these lessons, at national and international levels?

This brings the argument right back to our starting point: the question of the interrelationships between community action and the broad Labour movement, including both the trade union movement and the formal political structures. How can these interrelationships be developed as part of the longer-term construction of a popular climate of support for radical social change?

It is no part of our argument that this kind of change can be brought about easily or quickly. Our case study material has shown that achievements can be made in terms of getting people to work together more effectively and also in making improvements in their local situation. It has also shown that such work requires time and dedication and a belief in its continuing existence.

Of course, the ideal of self-help and voluntary activity is not the prerogative of any one political ideology. Indeed both the Conservative Party and the new Liberal/Democratic Alliance have shown significant interest in arguing for an increase in voluntary effort to go alongside of/as a substitute for public services. Such effort, however, would be devoted to maintaining the established structural arrangements and the underlying views which sustain them. Our concern has been, on the contrary, with the potential of community action in the development of alternative strategies for tackling the present economic and social crisis.

References

Introduction   Socialism and community action

1 From the research brief presented by the Gulbenkian Foundation.
2 See J. Hanmer and H. Rose, 'Making sense of theory', in P. Henderson, D. Jones and D. Thomas (eds), *The Boundaries of Change in Community Work*, London, Allen & Unwin, 1980.
3 See A. Sivanandan, *A Different Hunger: Writings on Black Resistance*, London, Pluto Press, 1982.

Chapter one   The community action movement and party politics

1 T. Bottomore, *Political Sociology*, London, Hutchinson, 1979.
2 D. Butler and D. Kavanagh, *The British General Election of 1974*, London, Macmillan, 1974.
3 *Putting Britain First*, Conservative Party, September 1974.
4 *Britain Will Win With Labour*, Labour Party, September 1974.
5 *Why Britain Needs a Liberal Government*, Liberal Party, September 1974.
6 *The Times*, October 1974.
7 D. Webster, *The Labour Party and the New Left*, London, Fabian Society, 1981.
8 T. Benn, 'Question and Answer', *New Socialist*, October 1981.
9 R. Mckenzie, *British Political Parties*, London, Mercury Books, 1964.
10 T. Benn, *Arguments for Socialism*, London, Cape, 1979.
11 D. Healey, 'Question and Answer', *New Socialist*, October 1981.
12 D. Kogan and M. Kogan, *The Battle for the Labour Party*, London, Fontana, 1982.
13 E. Hobsbawm, *The Forward March of Labour Halted*, London, Verso, 1981.
14 E. Lockwood and J. Goldthorpe, *The Affluent Worker in the Class Structure*, Cambridge University Press, 1969.
15 Quoted in the *Daily Telegraph*, 29 March 1979.

16 D. Marquand, *'Russet Coated Captains': The Challenge of Social Democracy*, Open Forum SDP, 1982.

17 F. Gripps, J. Griffiths, F. Morrell, J. Reid, P. Townsend, S. Weir, *Manifesto: A Radical Strategy for Britain's Future*, London, Pan, 1981.

18 For useful introductory discussion see C. Boggs, *Gramsci's Marxism*, London, Pluto Press, 1976.

19 M. Ward, 'Job Creation by the Council', *Local Government and the Struggle for Full Employment*, Workers' Control, 1981.

20 D. Bull, *Action for Welfare Rights*, London, Fabian Society, 1970.

21 T. Lynes, *Welfare Rights*, London, Fabian Society, 1969.

22 CDP, *Interproject Report*, London, Centre for Environmental Studies, 1974.

23 Coventry Workshop, 1977.

24 Calouste Gulbenkian Foundation, *Current Issues in Community Work*, London, Routledge & Kegan Paul, 1973.

Chapter two   Community action and political theory

1 D. Donnison with P. Soto, *The Good City: A Study of Urban Development and Policy in Britain*, London, Heinemann, 1980, Chapter 2, and D. Donnison, *The Politics of Poverty*, London, Martin Robertson, 1982.

2 P. Henderson, D. Jones and D. Thomas (eds), *The Boundaries of Change in Community Work*, London, Allen & Unwin, 1980, Introduction.

3 D. Corkey and G. Craig, 'CDP: community work or class politics', in P. Curno (ed.), *Political Issues and Community Work*, London, Routledge & Kegan Paul, 1978, pp. 36-66.

4 S. Hatch, *Outside the State: Voluntary Organisations in Three English Towns*, London, Croom Helm, 1980.

5 C. Cockburn, *The Local State: Management of Cities and People*, London, Pluto Press, 1977.

6 S. Bolger, P. Corrigan, J. Docking and N. Frost, *Towards Socialist Welfare Work*, London, Macmillan, 1981.

7 M. Mayo, 'The history and early development of CDP', in R. Lees and G. Smith (eds), *Action Research in Community Development*, London, Routledge & Kegan Paul, 1975.

8 C. Pateman, *Pariticipation and Democratic Theory*, Cambridge University Press, 1970.

9 S. Bolger *et al.*, *op. cit.*

10 J. O'Malley, *The Politics of Community Action*, Nottingham, Spokesman Books, 1977.

11 C. Ward, 'Stand', *New Society*, 4 December 1980, p. 471.

12 P. Taylor-Gooby, 'The New Right and social policy', in *Critical Social Policy*, vol. 1, no. 1, 1981.

13 London Edinburgh Weekend Return Group, *In and Against the State*, London, Black Rose Press, 1979.

14 L. Althusser, 'Ideology and ideological state apparatuses', in *Lenin and Philosophy and other Essays*, London, New Left Books, 1971.

15 J. Cowley, *Housing for People or for Profit?*, London, Stage One, 1979.

16 The focus for example of G. Craig, N. Derricourt and M. Loney, *Community Work and the State – Towards a Radical Practice*, London, Routledge & Kegan Paul, 1982.

17 D. Corkey and G. Craig, *op. cit.*

18 T.R. Batten and M. Batten, *The Non-Directive Approach in Group and Community Work*, Oxford University Press, 1967.

19 R. Leaper, *Community Work*, London, National Council of Social Service, 1968.

20 J. Lambert, 'Political values and community work practice', in P. Curno (ed.), *op. cit.*, pp. 3-16.

21 J. Smith, 'Hard lines and soft options: a criticism of some left attitudes to community work', in P. Curno (ed.), *op. cit.*, pp. 17-35.

22 J. Cowley, 'The politics of community organising', in J. Cowley, A. Kaye, M. Mayo, M. Thompson, *Community or Class Struggle*, London, Stage One, 1977, p. 235.

23 J. Cowley, *op. cit.*, p. 235.

24 A. Gortz, 'A strategy for labour', reprinted in J. Cowley *et al.*, *op. cit.*, p. 37.

25 M. Mayo, 'Community development: a radical alternative?', in R. Bailey and M. Brake (eds), *Radical Social Work*, London, Edward Arnold, 1975.

26 C. Cockburn, *op. cit.*

27 E. Wilson, *Women and the Welfare State*, London, Tavistock, 1977.

28 For an account of these debates see M. Harloe, 'New perspectives in urban and regional research: progress and problems', in M. Harloe (ed.), *New Perspectives in Urban Change and Conflict*, London, Heinemann, 1981, pp. 1-26.

29 L. Althusser, *Reading Capital*, London, New Left Books, 1970.

30 London Edinburgh Weekend Return Group, *op. cit.*

31 S. Jacobs, 'The sale of council houses: does it matter?', *Critical Social Policy*, vol. 1, no. 2, 1981, pp. 35-53.

32 P. Leonard, 'Restructuring the welfare state', *Marxism Today*, December 1979.

33 M. Harloe, *op. cit.*

34 P. Taylor-Gooby, 'The new right and social policy', in *Critical Social Policy*, vol. 1, no. 1, 1981.

35 K. Coates and R. Silburn, *Poverty: the Forgotten Englishman*, London Penguin, 1970.

36 G. Craig, M. Mayo and N. Sharman, *Jobs and Community Action*, London, Routledge & Kegan Paul, 1979.

37 P. Saunders, 'Community power, urban managerialism and the "local state" ', in M. Harloe (ed.), *op. cit.*, pp. 27-49.

38 S. Kennett and P. Hall, 'The inner city in spacial perspective', in P. Hall (ed.), *The Inner City in Context*, London, Heinemann, 1981.

39 D. B. Massey and R. A. Meegan, 'Industrial restructuring versus the cities', *Urban Studies*, 15, 1978, pp. 272-88.

40 Community Development Project, 'The costs of industrial change', 1977.

41 P. Taylor-Gooby, 'The new right and social policy', *Critical Social Policy*, vol. 1, no. 1, 1981.

42 L. Chalker, 'We are richer than we think', London, Conservative Party pamphlet, undated.

43 Letter from Secretary of State to leaders of Inner City Partnership and Programme Authorities, July 1981.

44 D. Saville, 'Negotiating a new tenancy agreement', in L. Smith and D. Jones (eds), *Deprivation, Participation and Action*, London, Routledge & Kegan Paul, 1981.

45 S. Hatch, *op. cit.*

46 J. Gershuny, *After Industrial Society: the Emerging Self-Service Economy*, London, Macmillan, 1978.

47 Lord Beveridge, *Voluntary Action*, London, Allen & Unwin, 1948, p. 10.

48 G. Jones, 'South Hereford', in R. Hadley and M. McGrath, *Going Local*, NCVO Occasional Paper 1, London, Bedford Square Press, 1980, p. 16.

49 R. Hadley and S. Hatch, *Social Welfare and the Failure of the State: Centralised Social Services and Participatory Alternatives*, London, Allen & Unwin, 1981.

50 M. Loney, 'Policies for community care in the context of mass unemployment', in G. Craig, N. Derricourt and M. Loney (eds), *Community Work and the State*, London, Routledge & Kegan Paul, 1982.

51 P. Henderson and D. Thomas, *Skills in Neighbourhood Work*, London, Allen & Unwin, 1980, p. 1.

52 P. Henderson, D. Jones and D. Thomas (eds), *The Boundaries of Change in Community Work*, London, Allen & Unwin, 1980.

53 S. Bolger *et al.*, *op. cit.*

54 M. Mayo, 'Community action programmes in the early eighties: what future?', *Critical Social Policy*, vol. 1, no. 3, 1982, pp. 5-18.

55 B. Hindess, *Parliamentary Democracy and Socialist Politics*, London, Routledge & Kegan Paul, 1983.

56 P. Corrigan and P. Leonard, Social Work Practice Under Capitalism:
a Marxist Approach, London, Macmillan, 1978.
57 M. Jaggi, R. Muller and S. Schmid, Red Bologna, Writers and
Readers Publishing Co-operative Society, 1977.
58 E. Lebas, 'The new school of urban and regional research: into the
second decade', in M. Harloe and E. Lebas (eds), City, Class and
Capital, London, Edward Arnold, 1981.
59 Since this chapter was first written however, War on Want's UK
programme has unfortunately been seriously affected by financial
difficulties.

Chapter three   Community action and anti-poverty programmes

1 H. Salmon, 'Ideology and practice', in P. Curno (ed.), Political Issues
and Community Work, London, Routledge & Kegan Paul, 1978, p.
67.
2 J. Smith, 'Hard lines and soft options', in P. Curno (ed.), op. cit.
3 The concern, for example of G. Craig, N. Derricourt and M. Loney
(eds), Community Work and the State: Towards a Radical Practice,
London, Routledge & Kegan Paul, 1982.
4 E. James, 'From Paris to ESCAP: the European anti-poverty
programme 1972-81', Community Development Journal, vol. 16, no.
2, April 1981.
5 V. George and R. Lawson, Poverty and Inequality in Common
Market Countries, London, Routledge & Kegan Paul, 1980, pp. 233-
4.
6 H. Delecck, 'Où va la sécurité sociale', Revue Belge de Sécurité
Sociale, 1971, p. 15, quoted in J. Berghman, 'Poverty and Inequality
in Belgium', in George and Lawson (ed.), op. cit.
7 V. George and R. Lawson, op. cit.
8 P. Townsend, Poverty in the United Kingdom, London, Penguin,
1979.
9 E. James, op. cit.
10 F. Piven and R. Cloward, Regulating the Poor, London, Tavistock,
1972.
11 S. Alinsky, '1965, The war on poverty: political pornography',
Journal of Social Issues, January 1965, pp. 41-7.
12 George and Lawson, op. cit.
13 Final Report, National Committee on Pilot Schemes to Combat
Poverty, Dublin, 1980, p. 36.
14 P. Jackson, unpublished paper, Dublin, 1980.
15 P. Jackson, ibid.
16 The Network of Labour, Community Research and Resources
Centres Prospectus, 1981/2.

17 SWAPAC Progress Report, 1978-9.
18 *Ibid.*
19 *Ibid.*

Chapter four   Information, advocacy and community action

1 Gulbenkian Foundation, *Community Work and Social Change*, London, Longmans, 1958.
2 A. Skeffington, *People and Planning*, London, HMSO, 1969.
3 C. Wright Mills, *The Power Elite*, Oxford University Press, 1956, p. 300.
4 Wright Mills, *ibid.*, p. 323.
5 R. Miliband, *The State in Capitalist Society*, London, Weidenfeld & Nicolson, 1969, p. 220.
6 Miliband, *ibid.*, p. 221.
7 Miliband, *ibid.*, p. 227.
8 Trade Union Congress Media Working Group, 'A Cause for Concern', London, TUC, 1979.
9 Glasgow University Media Group publications include most recently *Really Bad News*, London, Writers and Readers Publishing Co-operative Society, 1982.
10 Similar arguments about the role of the media were made earlier, too, for example, S. Hall, 'The structured communication of events', revised and updated in D. Potter *et al.* (eds), *Society and the Social Sciences*, London, Routledge & Kegan Paul, 1981; originally called 'Getting the Message', Paris, Unesco, 1965.
11 R. Williams (ed.), *May Day Manifesto*, London, Penguin, 1968, p. 40.
12 Source: *Social Trends*, London, HMSO, 1980.
13 *Directory of Social Change*, London, Community Publishers, 1977, p. 175.
14 *Community Action*, no. 27, 1976.
15 M. Meacher, 'Whitehall's short-way with democracy', in K. Coates (ed.), *What Went Wrong?: Explaining the Fall of the Labour Government*, Nottingham, Spokesman, 1979.
16 E. P. Thompson, *Writing by Candlelight*, London, Merlin, 1980.
17 H. Butcher, I. Cole and A. Glen, 'Information and action services for rural areas', *Journal of Social Policy*, no. 5,
18 N. Bond, *The Hillfields Information and Opinion Centre: the evaluation of a social agency controlled by local residents*, CDP Occasional Paper, Coventry, 1972.
19 T. Simpson, *Advocacy and Social Change*, National Institute of Social Work Papers, no. 8, 1978.

20 B. Wootton, *Social Science and Social Pathology*, London, Allen & Unwin, 1959.
21 A. Sinfield, *Which Way Social Work?*, London, Fabian Society, 1969.
22 H. Kutchins and S. Kutchins, 'Advocacy and social work', in G. Weber and H. McColl (eds), *Social Scientists as Advocates: Views from the Applied Disciplines*, London, Sage Publications 1978, p. 43.
23 P. Davidoff and D. Davidoff, 'Advocacy and urban planning', in G. Weber and H. McColl (eds), *op. cit.*
24 US Department of Health, Education and Welfare, 1967.
25 K. Bell, *Research Study on Supplementary Benefits Appeal Tribunals*, London, HMSO, 1975.
26 H. Rose, 'Who can delabel the claimant?', *Social Work Today*, vol. 4, no. 31, 1973.
27 N. Bond, *op. cit.*
28 'Community work service', report to the Inner London Education Authority, 1979/80.
29 Community Work Service, 'Community health work in the Inner City: the London experience', (unpublished) 1980.
30 Community Work Service, progress report to the EEC, 1978/79.
31 Supplementary Benefits Commission Annual Report, HMSO, Cmnd 6910, 1976.
32 Social Security Act 1980, HMSO, 1980.
33 M. Zander, *Legal Services for the Community*, London, Temple, 1978, p. 318.
34 J. Luba, 'Tribunal assistance schemes in England and Wales', LLM thesis, University of Leicester, 1980.

Chapter five   Employment

1 Department of Employment, *Employment Gazette*, vol. 90, no. 9, 1982.
2 CDP, 'Gilding the ghetto', 1977, p. 53.
3 CDP, 'Gilding the ghetto', *ibid.*, p. 26.
4 CDP, 'The costs of industrial change', 1977.
5 CDP, 'The costs of industrial change', *ibid.*
6 D. Corkey and G. Craig, 'CDP – community work or class politics?', in P. Curno (ed.), *Political Issues and Community Work*, London, Routledge & Kegan Paul, 1978, p. 36.
7 See Chapter Two, page 27.
8 Inner Area Studies Report, Department of the Environment, 1977.
9 P. Walker, 'The political framework – a conservative view', in M. Loney and M. Allen (eds), *The Crisis of the Inner City*, London, Macmillan, 1979.
10 B. Davis and J. Green, 'Inner city policy: A Marxist comment', in M.

Loney and M. Allen (eds), *ibid.*

11 'State intervention in industry: a workers' enquiry', Coventry, Liverpool, Newcastle, North Tyneside Trades Councils, 1980.

12 P. Hall (ed.), *The Inner City in Context: Retrospect and Prospect*, London, SSSRC, 1981.

13 M. Ward, 'Job-creation by the council: local government and the struggle for full employment', in *Workers' Control*, 1981, no. 3, p. 10.

14 'Newcastle-upon-Tyne trades council's centre for the unemployed,' paper produced by the Newcastle Centre.

15 Newcastle-upon-Tyne Trades Council, *ibid.*

16 TUC 'Unemployment: the fight for TUC alternatives', London, 1981.

17 I. Breugel, 'Women as a reserve army of labour: a note on recent British experience', *Feminist Review*, 1979, no. 3.

18 J. Dromey and G. Taylor, *Grunwick: the Workers' Story*, London, Lawrence & Wishart, 1978.

19 Chapters by M. Riley, 'A women's employment group in Milton Keynes', London Women's Employment Projects and A. Boyle, 'Job sharing: a new pattern in employment', in *Women in Collective Action*, A. Curno (ed.), A. Lamming, L. Leech, J. Stiles, V. Ward and T. Ziff, ACW, 1982.

20 London Women's Employment Projects in A. Curno (ed.), A. Lamming *et al.*, *op. cit.*

21 GARC, First Annual Report, October 1977.

22 *Ibid.*

23 *Ibid.*

24 GARC, Second Annual Report, November 1978.

25 *Ibid.*

26 Personal interview for the evaluation process.

27 GARC, Second Annual Report, *op. cit.*

28 *Ibid.*

29 GARC Annual Report, 1979.

30 SWAPAC Progress Report, part II, 1976.

31 *Ibid.*

32 *Ibid.*

33 *Ibid.*

34 *Ibid.*

35 *Ibid.*

36 SWAPAC Progress Report, 1978-9.

37 *Ibid.*

38 *Ibid.*

39 *Ibid.*

40 *Ibid.*

41 *Ibid.*

42 *Ibid.*

Chapter six Housing and planning

1 For example, P. Ambrose and R. Colenutt, *The Property Machine*, Harmondsworth, Penguin, 1975; T. A. Broadbent, *Planning, Profit and the Urban Economy*, London, Methuen, 1977; C. Cockburn, *The Local State*, London, Pluto Press, 1977; P. Dunleavy, *Urban Political Analysis*, London, Macmillan, 1980; and O. Marriott, *The Property Boom*, London, Hutchinson, 1967 – to mention only a few.
2 For example, S. Jacobs, *The Right to a Decent House*, London, Routledge & Kegan Paul, 1976, describes the community action which arose in response to such a clearance scheme in Glasgow.
3 Described for example in J. Cowley's account of private tenants' struggle for municipalisation in Camden, London in J. Cowley, *Housing for People or Profit?*, London, Stage One, 1979.
4 M. Castells, *The Urban Question*, London, Edward Arnold, 1977.
5 M. Harloe (ed.), *Captive Cities: Studies in the Political Economy of Cities and Regions*, London, Wiley, 1977.
6 See e.g., J. Westergarad, 'The rent strikes of 1968', in R. Millband and J. Savile, *Socialist Register*, London, Merlin, 1972.
7 J. Cowley, A. Kaye, M. Mayo, M. Thompson, *Community or Class Struggle*, London, Stage One, 1977, for example, discusses the development of both community work and community action in terms of these processes.
8 At this point, the groups included N. Southwark CD Group, Battersea Riverside Action Group, Covent Garden CA and the Fitzrovia Neighbourhood Association – the last two groups having joined in 1977.
9 GLC Planning Committee Report, 1982.

Conclusion The way forward

1 J. S. Mill, *Essays on Politics and Culture*, Himmelfarb, G. (ed.), New York, 1963, p. 186.
2 Quoted in B. Burke, *Rebels with a Cause: the History of Hackney Trades Council 1900-1975*, Hackney Trades Council and Hackney Workers' Educational Association, 1975, p. 28.
3 A. Sivanandan, 'From resistance to rebellion', in *A Different Hunger: Writings on Black Resistance*, London, Pluto Press, 1982.

Index